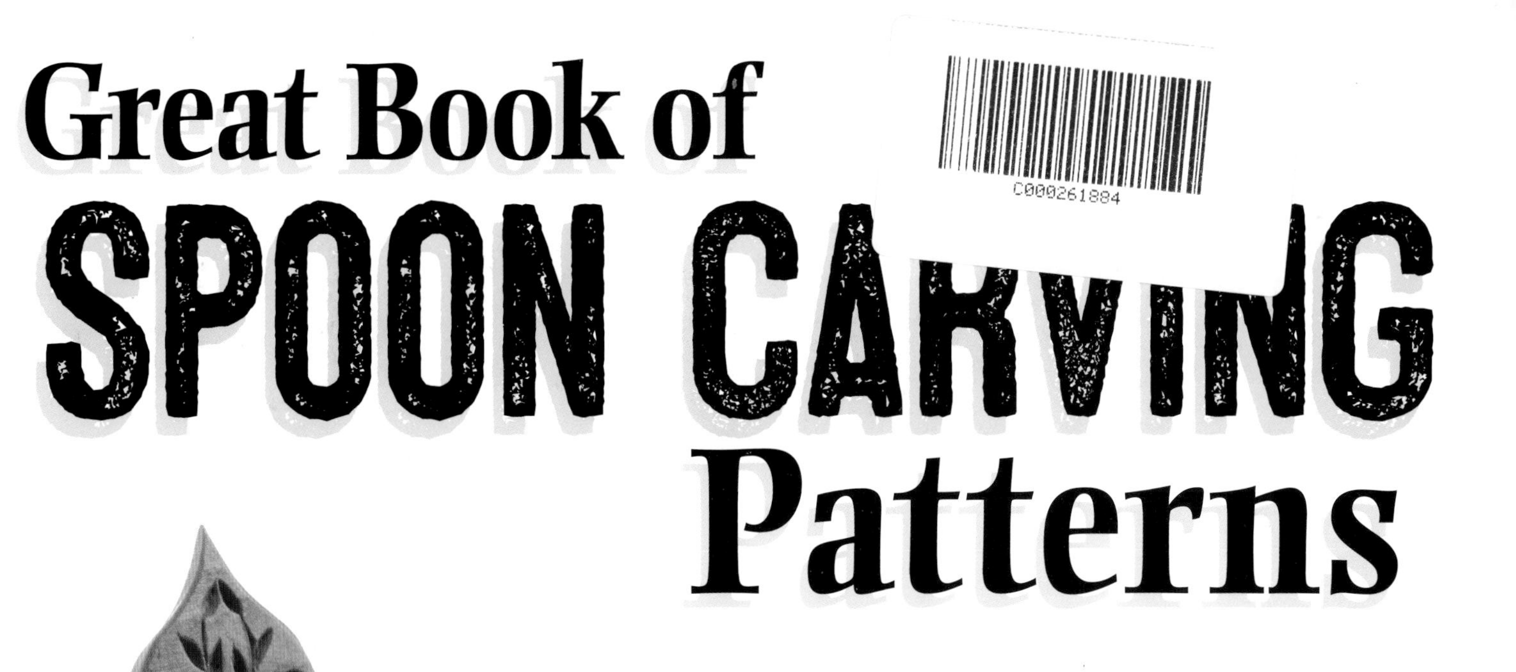

Great Book of SPOON CARVING Patterns

Detailed Patterns & Photos
for Decorative Spoons

DAVID WESTERN

FOX CHAPEL
PUBLISHING

Photography © Chris Roberts, Victoria BC Canada
Supplemental Photography © Fox Chapel Publishing by Mike Mihalo

ISBN 978-1-4971-0151-7

Library of Congress Control Number: 2020947119

To learn more about the other great books from Fox Chapel Publishing, or to find a retailer near you, call toll-free 800-457-9112 or visit us at *www.FoxChapelPublishing.com.*

We are always looking for talented authors. To submit an idea, please send a brief inquiry to acquisitions@foxchapelpublishing.com.

Printed in Singapore
First printing

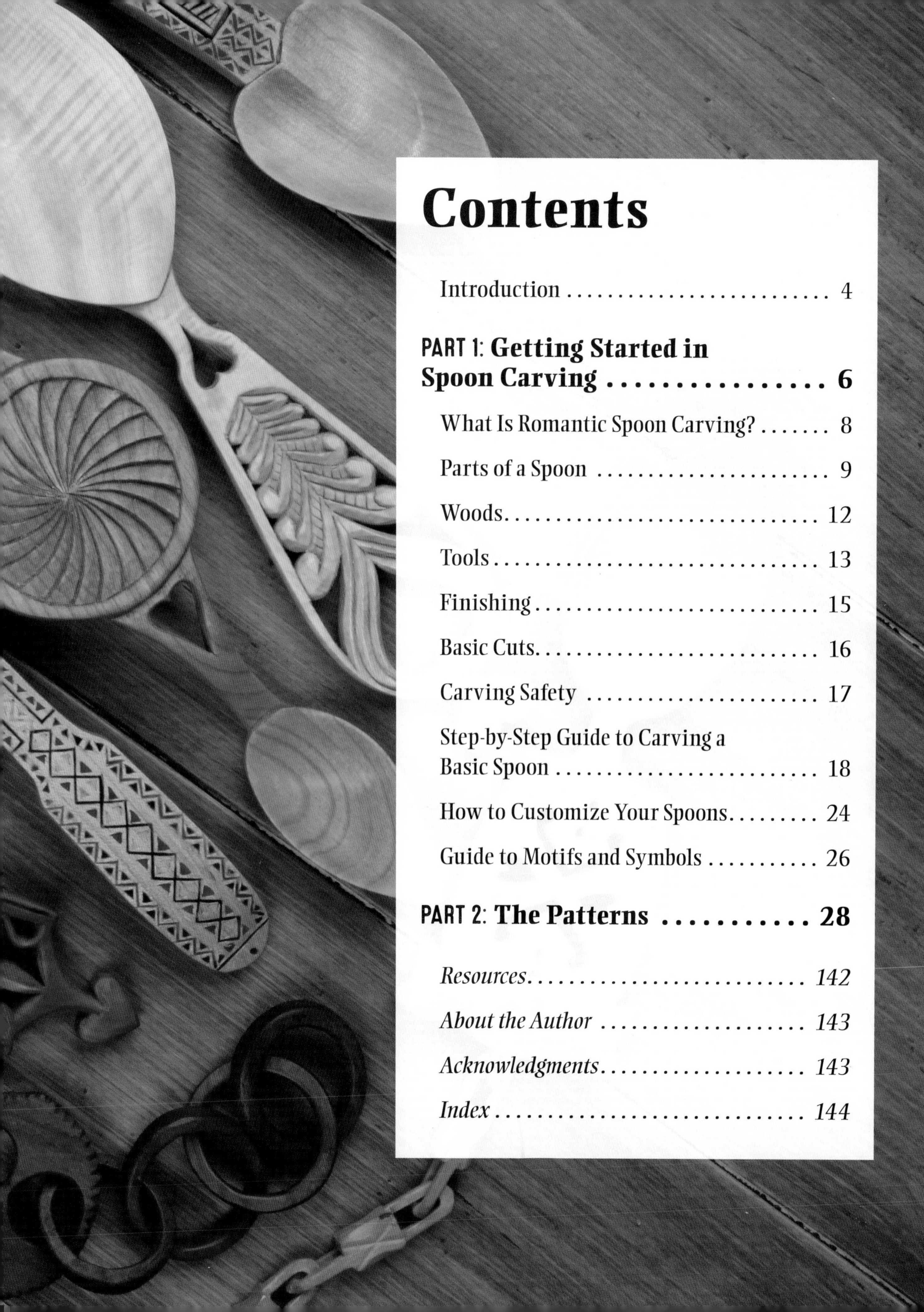

Contents

Introduction 4

PART 1: Getting Started in Spoon Carving 6

What Is Romantic Spoon Carving? 8

Parts of a Spoon 9

Woods. 12

Tools 13

Finishing 15

Basic Cuts. 16

Carving Safety 17

Step-by-Step Guide to Carving a Basic Spoon 18

How to Customize Your Spoons. 24

Guide to Motifs and Symbols 26

PART 2: The Patterns 28

Resources. 142

About the Author 143

Acknowledgments. 143

Index 144

Introduction

Spoons are more than just functional utensils that you use and then toss into the dishwasher. If you've never heard of decorative or romantic spoons, this book will teach you the basics about this exciting tradition. Even if you already know a bit about the topic, this book will expand your horizons with great recommendations for carving and finishing. It will also equip you with all the information you need to make your own historically inspired and unique romantic spoons.

Any spoon that is not meant for eating but for display or gifting is a decorative spoon, but not all decorative spoons are romantic spoons. A romantic spoon cannot simply function as a utensil or as an attractive art piece; it must also send a message of feeling, passion, or love. Although such spoons are frequently and somewhat too broadly called "lovespoons," you will soon see that this is a restrictive name for a wide and rich field of spoon carving. This book's collection digs into that field, examining tester, courting, wedding, novelty, and festival spoons, and explains the variety of purposes for which these romantic spoons were historically (and are still today) given and used.

The spoons that make up this volume are historical facsimiles, designed to be accurate to period, region, and dominant styles. Many are amalgamations of a range of common features or techniques, while others more closely represent a particularly significant historical spoon or regional specialty style. They are not intended to be exact replicas, simply very accurate historical representations.

The patterns in this book can be directly copied and carved, but they can also be cut and pasted in new combinations of elements to create an infinite array of fresh designs. For those with strong design abilities, this book will provide a rich foundation on which to experiment and build.

Romantic spoon carving is a lot of fun and is a very worthwhile pursuit. Whether you wish to carve a wedding or anniversary gift, a birth or memorial marker, or if you just want to enjoy the technical challenge of carving some of the designs, you will find plenty of inspiration and assistance within these pages.

Dave Western

—David Western, BC, Canada

PART 1

Getting Started in Spoon Carving

This section will teach you everything you need to get started carving romantic spoons, including a quick introduction to their history and symbolism; suggested woods and essential tools; ways to finish and preserve your spoons; basic cuts and carving safety for novice carvers; how to customize a spoon design unique to you; and how to carve a basic spoon step by step. Read what applies to you based on your level of familiarity with spoon carving and woodcarving in general, then head to Part 2: The Patterns!

What Is Romantic Spoon Carving?

Beginning in the early to mid-1600s, it became common practice for young, single men throughout Europe to create ornately embellished, carved wooden love tokens that would be given as gifts to the young women who had caught their eye or captivated their hearts.

Often, these tokens tended to reflect regional trades, pastimes, or specialties by taking the form of decorated tools, with tools for knitting, lacework, or milking being particularly popular. In several regions, however, the spoon became the dominant courting, wedding, and gifting love token, eventually finding popularity from the Arctic Circle to the Carpathian Mountains.

Little is known of *why* the spoon became such a popular love token; explanations range from its simplicity to carve and its portability, to the urge of common folk to mimic the gentry's burgeoning use of fancy metal spoons.

The spoons themselves were given for a variety of romantic reasons, ranging from simple statements of passionate interest through to the symbolic sealing of marital unions. Ardent amateurs and impartial professionals alike carved them. Often, the spoon acted as a résumé, showing the young woman and her family that the young man was skilled and tenacious or that he was financially secure enough to afford the services of a professional. A well-carved spoon clearly showed the carver's abilities and his willingness to see a difficult task through to a proper conclusion, traits that were favorably viewed. However, a poorly carved offering would most certainly have not assisted the young man in winning approval with anyone.

Although the vast majority of romantic spoons are now carved by machinery in a commercial setting, more and more hand carvers are realizing just how wonderful a project they are. Easily crafted from limited materials and with a simple selection of tools, a spoon can encapsulate a great deal of symbolic imagery and tell a real story of love or admiration. They are beautifully suited as gifts for a wide range of circumstances ranging from weddings and anniversaries to birthdays and christenings.

Once carved only by men, now anyone can carve romantic spoons, and their range of purpose has expanded significantly with a vast array of symbolic images now utilized to make ever more meaningful designs. Whether you're a complete beginner or an advanced carver, spoon carving offers you an opportunity to create beautiful and deeply meaningful artwork from basic tools and minimal material.

Three antique Welsh lovespoons from the mid to late 19th century.

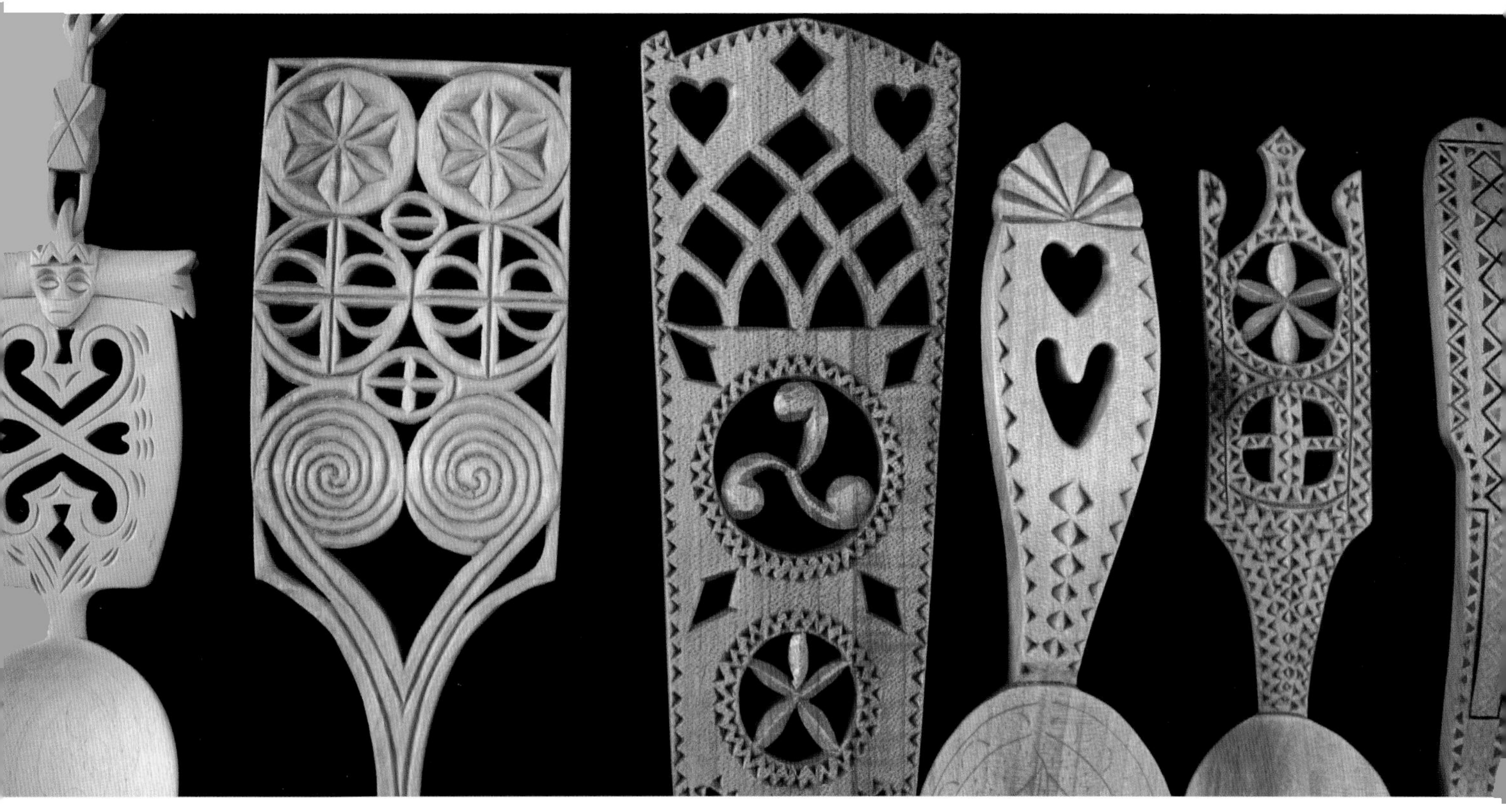

The variety of designs that can be found on a romantic spoon's handle is rich and infinite.

This Book's Goals

By creating this book, my intention is to fulfill three main goals. The first is to address two dismal shortages in the romantic spoon carving realm. Currently, there is an acute lack of published historical information regarding the romantic spoon, as well as an equally dire lack of spoon designs that are accurate to period and place; this book takes a large step toward filling that void.

The second goal is to give interested woodcarvers, artists, and enthusiasts an opportunity to study a mixture of design styles from the period of 1650–1900. It allows them to see firsthand the various techniques and styles used by the Northern European spoon carving community and to make their own versions of classic romantic spoon designs.

The third goal is to amply illustrate that the field of romantic spoon carving is much broader and richer than is often thought. Moving beyond the notion of all romantic spoons being "lovespoons," this collection delves into feeler, courting, wedding, novelty, and festival spoons and explains the variety of purposes for which romantic spoons were historically given and used.

Parts of a Spoon

HANDLES

The handle is the most noticeable part of a romantic spoon. It is the busy area where the romantic symbolism occurs and where the woodcarving artistry is on full display. Although modern spoons have become extremely complex and artistic, traditional romantic spoons relied on a much more limited design palette. That doesn't mean they were any less exuberant and passionate, though, and the craftsmen from each of the regions and countries highlighted in this book developed many unique and creative ways of decorating their spoons.

Detail of an exquisitely carved antique Welsh lovespoon.

STEMS

The stem area is found between the handle and the bowl and is an area outside of the bowl where carving was frequently undertaken on all faces and sides. Unlike today's typical souvenir lovespoons that are uniformly machined from flat timber, almost all antique romantic spoons employed curved stems to add dynamism and technical virtuosity to the designs.

A deeply sweeping stem adds tremendous visual drama to the spoon by enabling the spoon to cast a shadow when hung on the wall and helping the spoon to feel more comfortable when held in the hand.

As it is frequently the weakest section of the spoon, the timber in this section is often left deeper than it is wide. This gives the stem an elegant appearance when viewed from the front, but allows it to maintain maximum strength and support against breakage.

The sweep of the stem adds elegance and grace to a spoon's design.

BOWLS

The bowl was generally left unadorned on historical romantic spoons. However, that doesn't mean that it wasn't carefully and beautifully carved. Even on the crudest of antique spoons, an inordinate amount of time seems to have been spent ensuring the bowl was sleek and fair. Unlike modern souvenir spoons, the bowls on historical spoons were always elegant and refined with slender, delicate bowl walls and crisp, thin lips.

Historical spoon bowls appear light and dignified and offer a beautiful and serene counterpoint to the frequently busy handle designs. A spoon bowl is often tilted from its tip back toward the junction with the stem. This gives the spoon more visual vitality and is a clear indication to anyone viewing the spoon that the carver possessed both great skill and tremendous patience.

The bowl is the unsung part of the romantic spoon's magic and is frequently overlooked or mishandled by modern carvers. A poorly carved bowl can completely undercut any hard work that has gone into the handle and stem and leave a spoon looking amateurish and unfinished. Carving a balanced and elegant bowl is perhaps the best way to create a romantic spoon that is memorable and worthwhile!

A well-carved bowl is key to the success of a spoon's design.

Save for some occasional arching, the back face of antique romantic spoon handles was rarely decorated.

BACK SIDES

Traditionally, most romantic spoons were designed to be viewed from the front; they were commonly displayed hung on a wall or contained in a spoon rack. Although many carvers in the modern era like to finish both sides of the spoon's handle, in the old days they were most frequently left completely unadorned and unfinished. In many cases, the back surface was only crudely carved and the edges were not rounded over in any way.

Occasionally, by tapering from the center line toward the outer edges, carvers would coarsely shape the back to create an illusion of elegance and thinness when the spoon was viewed from the side. This technique enabled the carver to retain a good deal of robust structural integrity while giving the visual appearance of delicacy.

On many modern spoons, the backs are periodically used as a place to engrave names, dates, or romantic quotations, but this was extremely uncommon on historical examples. Most of the spoons in this volume feature little to no carving on their backs.

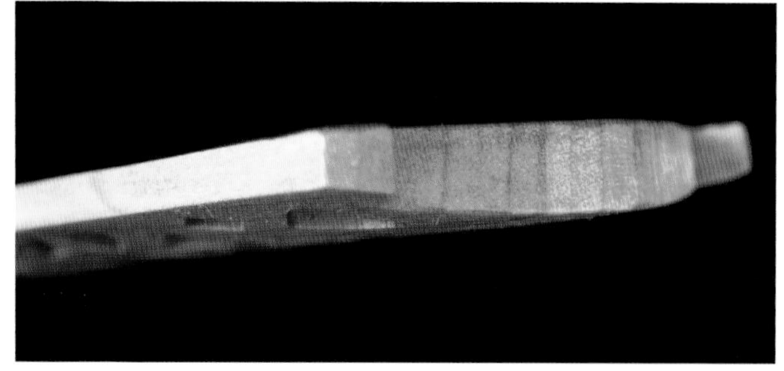

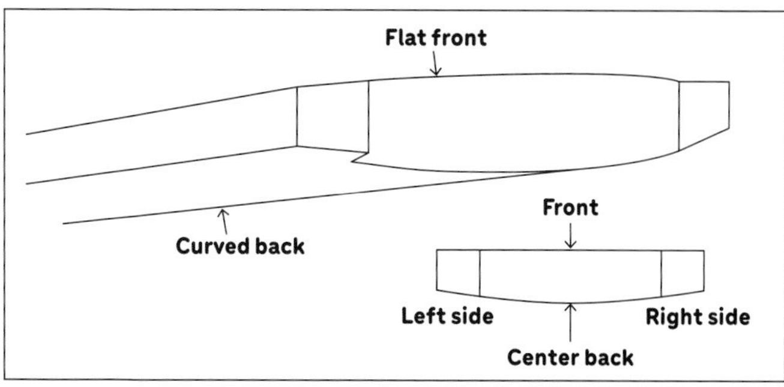

This close-up shows the gentle arch shaping of the handle's back surface. The top face of the spoon is flat; the bottom face of the spoon bows slightly outward from center, as you can see.

Woods

Each region of Europe has a species of tree that supplies carvers the main lumber for spoons carved in that area. The most popular woods tend to be deciduous (hardwood) timbers, which are on the softer end of the hardness scale while remaining sturdy enough to take detailing and withstand the forces of repetitive carving activity. Softwoods such as pines, fir, or cedars can also be used, but they have to be carefully selected, as they are frequently too soft and stringy for use as spoons.

For modern carvers wishing to emulate the woods of yore (detailed below), the most commonly available woods today are birch, linden, sycamore, bigleaf maple, red alder, cherry, and walnut. Boxwood and holly are good for smaller spoons that will be inlaid with wax, but these particular woods can be difficult to find, so fruitwoods and maple make a good substitute.

Generally, woods of lighter color tone and homogenous grain tend to be more suited for the elaborate detail common to romantic spoon carving. Woods with heavy grain patterns, such as oak and ash, can sometimes overwhelm delicate designs, so these are best used only for robust carvings.

In Scandinavia, the main wood used was birch, which, with its creamy coloration and even grain, is perfectly suited for the complex chainwork and intricate detailing so popular among carvers there. Birch cuts smoothly and rarely splinters, which makes it particularly suited for both bowl carving and incised detail work.

In Wales, the most popular wood for lovespoons was sycamore; it also features a light, creamy color and an even grain. Both birch and sycamore are relatively quick-growing species that were popular for fuel and were utilized to make everything from boxes to furniture.

The Bretons were celebrated for their remarkable and complex wax inlay work and so gravitated to denser and more homogenous woods, such as boxwood, apple, and cherry. These woods are harder and much more difficult to carve than birch and sycamore, but they cut extremely cleanly and leave the nice, smooth cuts that are so perfect for accommodating wax inlay.

In the Alpine regions of Europe, the classic woodcarvers' timber was linden (also known as lime in the UK and basswood in the US), but, at higher altitudes, several species of spruce and pine were also commonly carved. Birch grows in the lower regions and was also used for spoons and kitchen items.

Bigleaf maple | **Birch** | **Cherry** | **Eastern maple**

Pine | **Poplar** | **Red alder**

Tools

Although it is easy to get carried away when it comes to acquiring carving gear, it's important to remember that during the golden era of the romantic spoon, the vast majority of designs would have been carved with only the most basic of tools. Over the years, the growing accessibility of quality hand tools and the invention of power tools have changed everything for woodworkers of all stripes. Unfortunately and somewhat strangely, along with the ease and efficiency of machining seems to have come an equal loss of elegance and beauty. Today, the best spoons largely remain those crafted by hand, but this is not to say that power tools don't have a place in romantic spoon carving. As the Shakers discovered while building their remarkable furniture, machines can deal with the drudgery and monotony of many tasks, leaving the crafter more time and energy to devote to creating high-quality works of art.

Adze and axe

THE ESSENTIAL TOOLKIT

This simple collection of tools is similar to that which might have been available to farm workers from Wales and the Continent during the 1600s to 1800s. It will serve you just as well.

Straight knife: The straight knife is the tool most used in spoon carving. Whether used for rough-shaping, tidying, or the finest detail cutting, the straight knife is tremendously versatile. Larger knives are more suited to rapid stock removal, and smaller knives are most useful for detailing and delicate cutting. Most carvers will eventually accumulate a number of straight knives in a variety of lengths and shapes, but a good-quality knife approximately 1½ inches (3.8cm) in length with a finely pointed tip is an ideal tool to begin a collection.

Bent/hook knife: As the name implies, a bent knife has a curved blade that allows the cutting of concave surfaces. The ideal tool for shaping the spoon's bowl, it is a vital part of the toolkit and is very nearly as important as the straight knife. In Wales, carvers would often make their own bent knife blades from broken bucket handles, files, or scraps of metal from plowshares. On the Continent, the knives tended to be more of the hook knife style with a deeper and more circular blade shape. Either works fine and will also allow you to carve other detailing, such as textured surfaces, curved foliage, and deep hollows without the need for masses of expensive carving gouges.

Axe/adze: For removing stock rapidly and rough-shaping spoon blanks, there is no better hand tool than the axe. Although it is very much a learned skill and carries some inherent dangers, swinging an axe is an efficient and swift way to work wood during the initial stages of a carving. A straight-bladed axe will carry out the same functions as a straight knife, only on a much grander level. For concave

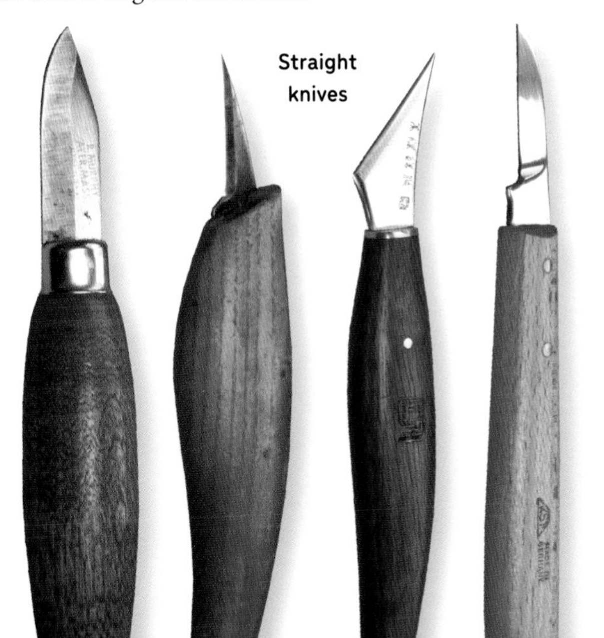

Straight knives

Bent/hook knives

cutting, such as shaping a curve into a handle or even rough-shaping a bowl, an adze is the perfect hand tool. Sometimes, it is possible to acquire a sculptor's adze that conveniently combines an axe and an adze on the same handle.

Sharpening stones/papers: To properly maintain cutting edges and ensure that all tools are in top working order, you must have some good-quality sharpening tools on hand. At the very minimum, a combination 1000X/4000X Japanese waterstone will keep tool edges refined and very sharp. Adding some super-fine paper abrasives that have been designed for tool sharpening allows for a very economical but highly efficient sharpening system. The addition of a leather strop and polishing paste will enable you to hone blades to a razor-sharp edge.

ADDITIONAL TOOLS

As mentioned earlier, it is easy to get carried away with tool purchases, especially when it comes to carving gouges and chisels. Rather than buy entire sets (most of which will remain in the box for years on end), buy tools on an as-needed basis. This will ensure a collection that is best suited for the type of work you do and will save a lot of money. **Gouges** are supremely useful for cutting concave surfaces and can be used to robustly remove stock or delicately shape fair surfaces from spoon bowls to flower petals. They exist in a bewildering array of widths and sweeps (the term for the curve of the blade). Begin your collection with a ½-inch (1.3cm)–wide shallow tool like a #5 sweep and a ½-inch (1.3cm)–wide deep tool like a #9 sweep, adding more shapes as you need them.

Two tools which are often overlooked but are ideal for spoon carving are the **file** and the **scraper**. Files allow you to undertake shaping and smoothing that would usually be done with sandpaper, allowing for a fine and clean surface free of sandpaper's microscopic grit particles that can dull cutting edges. Scrapers are another alternative to abrasives that enable the paring off of wafer-thin shavings from even the most difficult of wood grains.

There is no doubt that **power tools** have completely changed the face of woodcarving in the last 150 years. For rapid stock removal, nothing beats a **band saw**, a **scroll saw**, and a **drill press**. A band saw is ideal for milling down log lumber into useful carving billets and for rough-shaping the exterior lines of spoon patterns. A drill press can accurately drill away excess interior wood and allow for the easy threading of scroll saw blades for detail cutting. A scroll saw is probably the most versatile of the power tools for a spoon carver, allowing shaping of the blank, cutting of fine interior details, and, when fitted with a sanding attachment, power sanding.

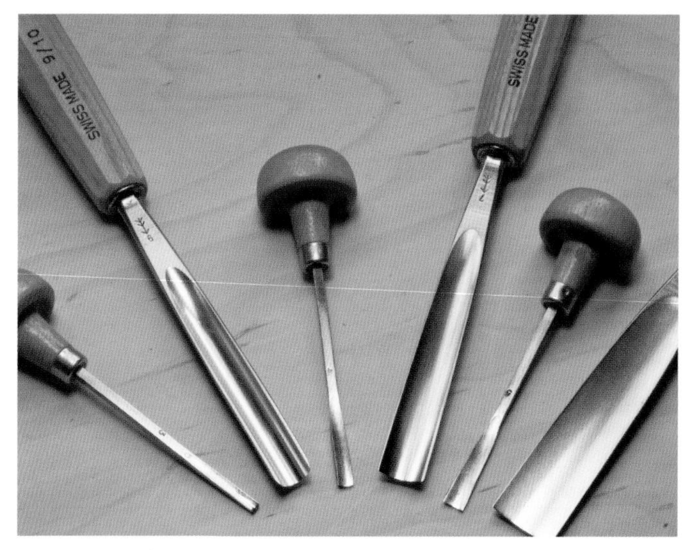

Gouges come in many shapes and sizes, but you will probably only require a select few for your spoon carving.

Scraper

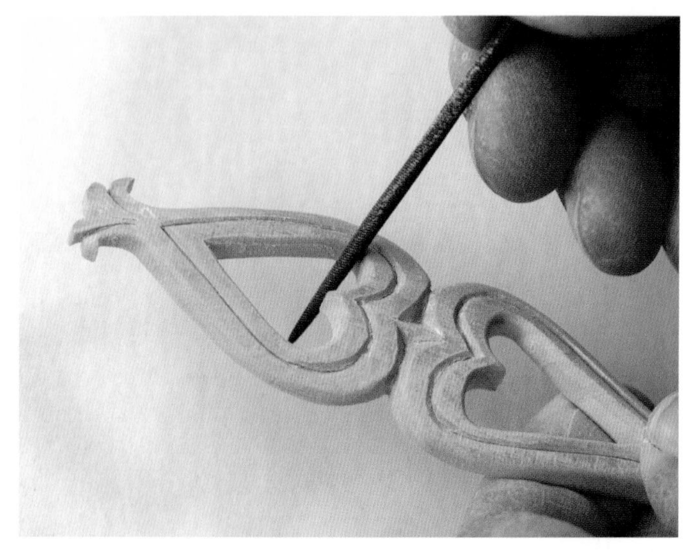

File

Finishing

Once you've completed a spoon, it will be time to consider whether or not to apply a finish.

Some spoons were left completely unfinished back in the old days and were allowed to develop the natural patina that comes from dust, dirt, and hand oils built up from years of handling. Others were given a variety of finish treatments ranging from beeswax or shellac to varnish or paint.

The purpose of a finish is to protect the carving against damage caused by dirt, dust, UV light, and oils. A finish can also "bring up" a wood's colors, grain, and figure and help the piece appear more vibrant and refined.

At their most basic level, finishes occur in two main types. **Film finishes** sit on the surface of the wood and are generally quite hard. As the name implies, they create a thin film that can be polished to a glossy shine. This type of finish is ideal for carvings with large, smooth surfaces, but it gets a bit too heavy and cloying for carvings with fine details. For richly carved surfaces, a **penetrating oil** is more suitable. This type of finish soaks into the wood surface and enhances the wood's colors more dramatically. It cannot be polished to a high gloss finish, but it can be buffed to the soft satin sheen more complementary to a detailed carving.

Whatever the finish, it will only be as good as the surface it is covering, so you must take great care to ensure the spoon has been thoroughly scraped, filed, or sanded before application. Any scratches, dents, or rough spots left on the carving will be immediately highlighted by the first coat of finish and will become very difficult to remove, so spend some time ensuring the carving is clean, crisp, and bright before finishing.

Because these spoons are not intended to be used for eating, a three- or four-coat **"Danish oil" style finish** (lightly sanded between coats with 1500-grit wet and dry abrasive) is a perfect finish. It protects the spoon, does not clog up fine detail work, and is easily applied and repaired. You can purchase Danish oil, or you can make a good homemade oil by combining ⅓ boiled linseed oil, ⅓ spar varnish or satin polyurethane, and ⅓ mineral spirits. Apply the finish with a small paintbrush until the entire spoon is well soaked. Leave for twenty minutes, then dry thoroughly with a clean, soft cotton rag. Repeat this process a second and third time, leaving 24 hours between each coat. After applying the final coat, lightly and gently sand the entire spoon with the 1500-grit abrasive to bring up a silky feel. Wipe dry and leave for a few days to thoroughly cure. Once the spoon is dry and the smell no longer lingers, buff the spoon with a nice finish coat of wax polish to bring up a soft sheen and impart a nice smell. Wet oil rags may spontaneously combust if not dealt with correctly, so follow the manufacturer's instructions for proper disposal.

For a food-safe finish, consider using mineral oil, 100% tung oil, or a commercial salad bowl preparation applied the same way as the Danish oil finish. If you want to use only a beeswax finish, be certain it is not a preparation containing potentially toxic drying/hardening agents.

Penetrating oil or beeswax polish finishes protect and enhance a finished spoon.

Basic Cuts

Like most types of carving, spoon carving is a subtractive art—you remove all of the material that isn't part of your vision for the final piece. Most carvers use four basic cuts to remove excess wood: the stop cut, the push cut, the paring cut, and the V-shaped cut. Master these four basic types of cuts and you'll be ready to tackle a multitude of projects.

STOP CUT

As the name suggests, the stop cut is used to create a hard line at the end of another cut. Your hand position depends on the placement of the cut you need to make. Regardless of your hand position, simply cut straight into the wood to create a stop cut. Make a stop cut first to prevent a consecutive cut from extending beyond the intended area. Make a stop cut second to free a chip of wood remaining from a primary cut.

PUSH CUT

For the push cut, hold the wood in one hand. Hold the knife in your other hand with the thumb on the back of the blade. Push the knife through the wood, away from your body. This type of cut is also called the straightaway cut. For additional control or power, place the thumb of the wood-holding hand on top of the thumb on the blade, and use the wood-holding thumb as a pivot as you rotate the wrist of your knife-holding hand. This maneuver is often called the thumb-pushing cut or lever cut.

PARING CUT

The paring cut gives you a great deal of control but requires you to cut toward your thumb. Wear a thumb protector or be aware of the knife position at all times, especially if it slips beyond the anticipated stopping point. To perform the paring cut, which is also called a draw cut, hold the wood in one hand. Hold the knife in the other hand with four fingers. The cutting edge points toward your thumb. Rest the thumb of your knife-holding hand on the wood behind the area you want to carve. Extend the thumb as much as possible. Close your hand, pulling the knife toward your thumb, to slice through the wood. This is the same action used to peel (or pare) potatoes.

V-SHAPED CUT

To make a V-shaped cut, hold a knife the same way you do when making a paring cut. Anchor the thumb of the knife hand against the wood and cut in at an angle with the tip of the knife. Rotate the wood, anchor your thumb on the other side of the cut, and cut in at an angle, running beside the first cut. Angle the two cuts so the bottom or deepest part of each cut meets in the center. This creates a V-shaped groove. Use the center of the cutting edge to make intersecting angled cuts on the corner of a blank, creating V-shaped notches.

Carving Safety

There is risk involved whenever you handle sharp tools. A knife sharp enough to cut through wood will easily cut skin. Most cuts are small nicks that heal quickly and don't leave a scar. However, it's best to follow simple safety procedures to prevent serious injuries.

The fundamental rule when it comes to spoon carving is to be aware not only of where the blade is, but where the blade could go. Wood can change density at any point, and you need to change the amount of pressure you apply on the knife based on the wood density. Imagine pushing hard to cut through a hard knot only to find a softer section of wood behind the knot. The sharp edge will quickly slice through the softer area and cut into whatever is in its path. The knife doesn't care if it's open air, a carving bench, or your hand.

Boy Scouts are taught to always cut away from themselves. While this is good advice, there are times when you cut toward your thumb, such as when making a paring cut (see page 16). When making a paring cut, wear a leather thumb protector, wrap your thumb with cloth tape, or position your thumb far enough down on the project so if the knife slips, it won't hit your thumb.

Because most cuts occur on the hand holding the project, carvers often wear a cut-resistant glove on that hand. It is possible to prevent cuts by being aware of where the sharp edge can (and probably will) go. Always cut away from yourself when you are removing bark or large amounts of wood. When you are carving finer details, anchor your holding hand to the carving hand. Place the thumb of your holding hand on the back of the thumb on the knife-holding hand when doing a push cut. Alternatively, rest the fingers of your knife hand on the fingers of your holding hand. Anchoring your hands adds stability and control, making it less likely that the knife will slip.

Some spoon carvers use their thighs as carving benches. A cut on your thigh can be serious. Carving on a workbench or table is recommended. If you cut toward your thigh, invest in a strip of leather to protect your leg.

Without proper precautions, a slip of the knife can result in a visit to the emergency room. Follow the above safety rules and you'll never require so much as a Band-Aid.

Learn more about this spoon and see the pattern on page 70.

Wear a glove on the hand holding your carving.

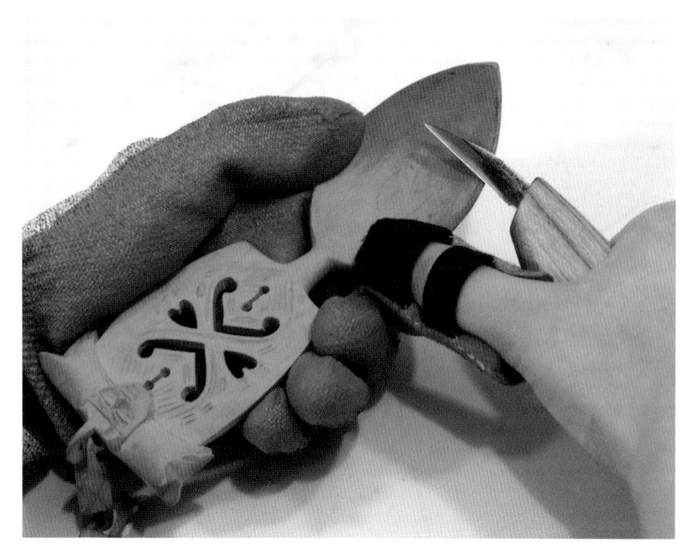

Wear a thumb guard when cutting toward your thumb.

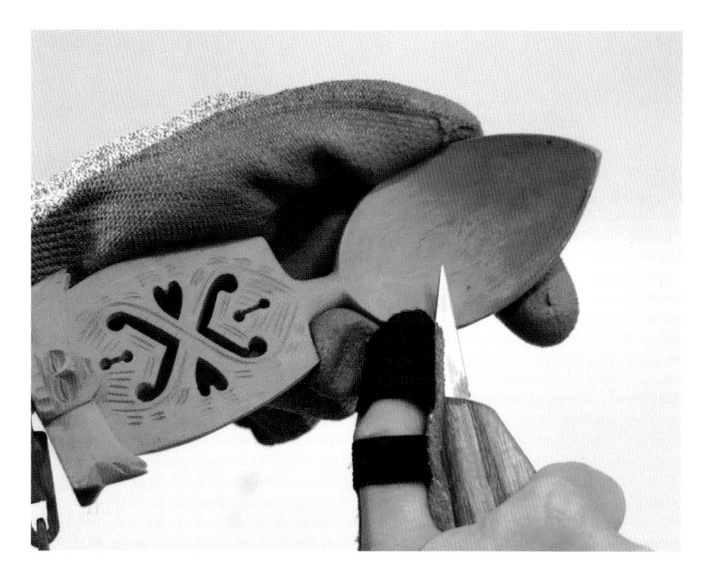

Cut away from yourself to prevent injury.

Step-by-Step Guide to Carving a Basic Spoon

Although this book is geared toward those who already have a basic working knowledge of woodcarving, this step-by-step guide will give newcomers, artists, and historians who may not have much carving experience the practice they need, and it will give any reader plenty of confidence before they tackle one of the patterns in this book. To carve this basic spoon, you'll just need the essential tools described in Tools earlier in this section. Follow along to make a simple, small Swedish "tester" spoon that you can be proud of. I carved mine from yellow cedar.

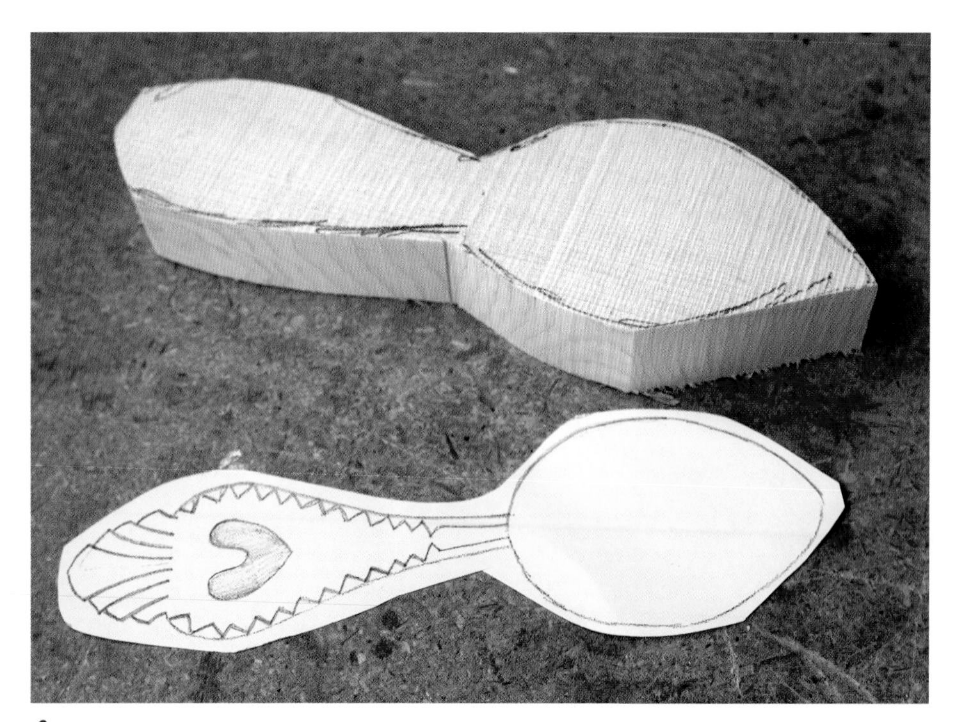

1 Select a pattern you'd like to carve and make a photocopy or tracing. Find a suitable piece of timber that will accommodate the pattern, keeping the wood's grain structure aligned in a straight line from the crown to the bowl tip if possible. Sketch the perimeter pattern onto the wood or apply it using transfer paper and a pencil. Once done, set the pattern photocopy aside for later use.

2 Use a band saw, jeweler's saw, axe, or straight knife to rough-cut the wood to size. With that completed, use the saw or axe/knife combination to rough-shape the bowl, stem, and handle.

Pattern at 100%

3 With the timber roughed out, use a rasp, scraper, plane, large chisel, or some files to shape a dome into the front face of the handle area. This will lend the finished spoon some movement and a more vibrant feel than a flat face would. If you don't have the tools to do the doming, leave the face flat; it will still look good!

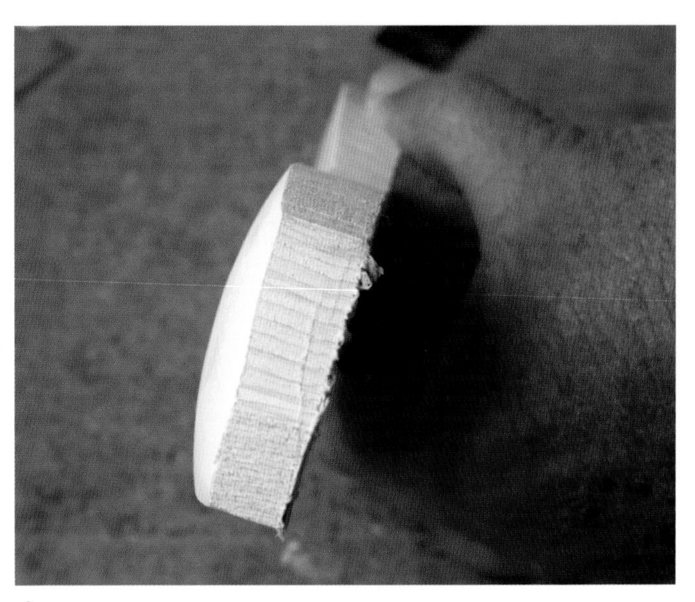

4 This picture shows the domed front face of the handle area. You can leave this area flat or exaggerate the dome even more if you wish. Go back over your work and make sure the domed area is uniformly smoothed to avoid any bumps or dips. The fairer the curves are, the nicer the finished spoon will look.

5 Attach the photocopied pattern to the block of wood using your preferred method; I use either repositionable spray adhesive or a glue stick. If you have domed the handle, be aware that the pattern has to be applied gently to avoid becoming creased. Cut to the lines using a band saw, scroll saw, jeweler's saw, or straight knife and elbow grease. Try to cut as neatly as possible, letting the blade do the work.

6 With the exterior lines all cut, begin removing any interior areas that must be cut away. Drill the holes for the interior areas, and then refine them with either the scroll saw or a knife. You can also use a jeweler's saw to effectively remove interior material. If you don't have a drill, scroll saw, or jeweler's saw, you can always use the tip of a straight knife to dig through the wood and clear these areas. When using a drill, I try to use the biggest bits possible to clear as much waste as I can before resorting to straight knives or saws.

7 Once the exterior and interior cutting is complete, begin shaping the spoon's bowl. Use gouges or a bent knife, being careful to not dig too deeply. Shallow, smooth cuts are infinitely preferable to deep cuts that may become ragged or even crack the bowl. Be conscious of how deep the bowl is getting, as it is easy to cut right through the timber and out the back! The neater the cutting is at this stage, the less work will be required to smoothly finish the bowl later.

8 Smooth the bowl. Although spoon bowls can be left "from the knife," I find that a really smooth bowl is more in keeping with the types of spoons found in museum collections. No doubt the young men who carved them wanted their spoons to be as close to perfect as they could get them, so they would have spent many hours burnishing them with bone or Dutch reed. Fortunately, we now have sandpaper, which, judiciously used, can save many hours of labor and leave behind a wonderfully fair and even spoon bowl.

9 With the front face of the spoon bowl complete, you can begin attending to the surface decorations on the handle. In this pattern, the design makes use of a repetitive triangular chip cut that can be performed with a straight knife. This kind of pattern requires consistency to be effective, so you'll need to concentrate on making all the cuts as similar in depth and width as possible. Rushing is the enemy of success, so enjoy the process and take as much time as you need.

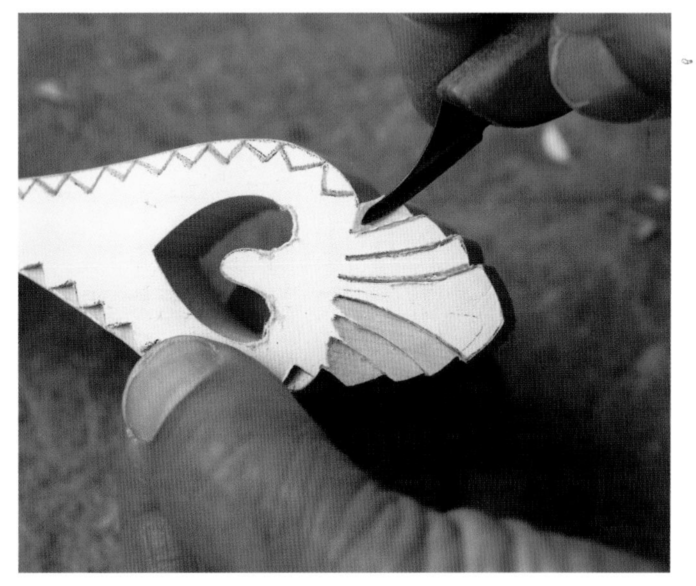

10 Complete the front of the handle. Details like the little fan at the crown of this spoon require particular care. Scribe all lines neatly with a straight knife before proceeding, then use a knife or chisel to carefully pare away the wood. When cutting "ramps" such as the ones that will create this fan, be careful to always follow the pattern forward, rather than back. This will enable you to cut toward uncut material at all times and will reduce the risk of chipping away the thin front edge of a finished ramp.

11 Once the front face of the handle has been carved, use a needle file, tightly rolled abrasive paper, or straight knife to clean up the edges of any interior cutouts. The neater you can make these edges, the better the spoon will look when the finishing oil is applied and the spoon is displayed. Files are preferable to sandpaper, as they cut rather than scratch and generally leave a much smoother and shinier surface.

12 To achieve a nice, rounded edge that dresses up your spoon, utilize a thin strip of fine cloth-backed abrasive to give the edges a fair and smooth look and feel. Use a light touch to ensure that you don't remove too much material and that what remains is as consistent as possible. Little discrepancies along edges are readily noticeable to the human eye, so regularity with the depth and width of any smoothed area is very important.

13 You'll want to leave the applied pattern on the spoon as long as possible, as it protects the surface from dirt and damage. Sometimes I'll leave it on until the very end, but I often remove it once the face carving is complete so that I know that the carving is as good as I can get it before proceeding to cut away the excess material on the back face. Make use of a scraper blade to remove the paper without any danger of scratching or cutting the wood beneath.

14 With the front face of the handle, stem, and bowl complete, it's time to begin shaping the back face of the bowl. This can be quickly achieved with a band saw, but a straight knife also works and has the added benefit of enabling you to work a bit more slowly and to feel the thickness of the remaining stock more closely.

15 Shape the area where the stem meets the bowl. Carve long facets to ensure that the curve remains fair and even without dips or rises. Here the facets have been cut by a band saw, so they are exaggerated but clearly visible for the camera. Further subdividing each facet gradually achieves the smooth curve that is required for an elegant bowl. The area where the handle joins the bowl needs to be kept as strong as possible, so shape carefully to achieve a graceful connection while maintaining structural integrity. I recommend leaving the stem area a bit deeper (thicker) than it is wide.

16 When you are satisfied that the bowl and stem are as gracefully carved as you can make them, give this area a thorough sanding with both cloth-backed and paper-backed abrasives. Aim to ensure all surfaces are as smooth and fair as possible with no divots or high points. Sand with the grain as much as possible to avoid cross-grain scratches, then ensure the lip of the bowl flows smoothly with a uniform thickness throughout. I generally begin sanding at 120-grit and work through to a final sanding at 320-grit.

17 Once the spoon is sanded down and is silky smooth with no scratches and blemishes, begin the finishing process. Because these spoons are decorative, you can make use of a Danish oil–type penetrating finish to protect the spoon from dust and dirt and to bring up the color of the wood grain. Wet sanding between coats using 1500-grit wet and dry abrasive paper gives the spoon a glassy, smooth feel; three to four coats is sufficient for most woods. Once the spoon has had time to cure, apply a final buffing of beeswax polish to bring up a nice satin sheen.

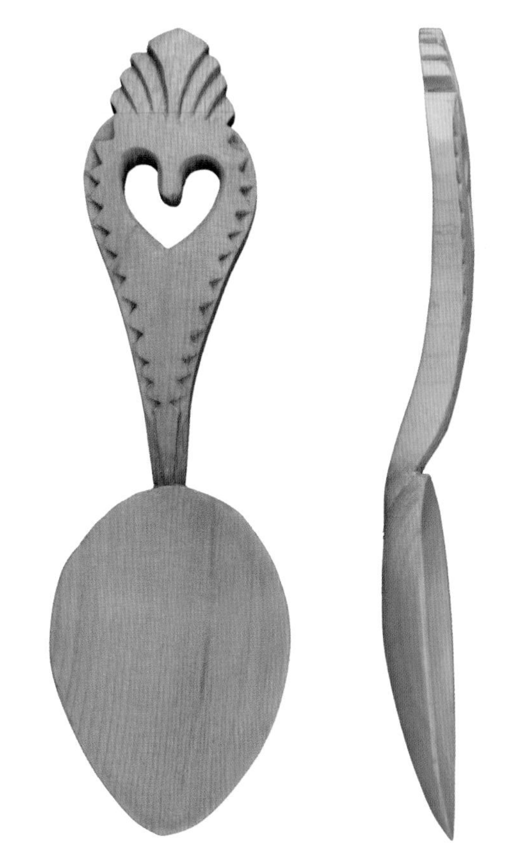

The finished spoon measures 7 inches (17.8cm) long, 2 inches (5cm) wide, and 1 inch (2.5cm) thick.

How to Customize Your Spoons

Although even the most enthusiastic of carvers could spend months working through the patterns presented in this book, for anyone wanting to create unique patterns of their own design, there is literally a lifetime's worth of design inspiration to be found here. Even if you have no artistic training, you can develop an infinite number of original ideas simply by cutting and pasting parts of different designs together and by experimenting with sizes and shapes. It's always astonishing how the simplest of alterations to a design can result in dramatic changes to a spoon's look, size, and feel.

Customizing a spoon's design need not be a difficult affair. Simple alterations to the size of its bowl or subtle variations in its handle shape can dramatically change the spoon's overall appearance. Using a very simple Swedish tester spoon for inspiration, the following photos show how a few simple modifications applied to a basic design can result in dramatically new "looks" for a spoon pattern. Any design can be adapted in this fashion, which opens up endless opportunity for creative exploration.

Perhaps the easiest place to make a dramatic alteration to a design is at the **bowl**. Some shapes naturally work better than others in matching a given handle, but frequently, a wide variety of bowl shapes will all work equally well. Try your designs with several different bowl sizes and shapes and see which ones work best. There is always a delicate balance to be sought between the bowl's size and shape and how it merges with the handle's form. As it's not always easy to get it just right, judge whether the bowl seems too wide or narrow, too long or short, and whether it's the right or wrong shape before committing to cutting the wood to size. Time spent tweaking a bowl's shape before carving is always time well spent.

The **handle** is generally the star of a romantic spoon, as it is the place where the eye is drawn and the message is sent. Here, there is literally infinite opportunity to

Simple variations can alter a design significantly. All three of these spoons have a similar fretwork, leafy look, but with different handle shapes, fret sizes, and bowl shapes and detailing, each one becomes unique.

experiment and play with design styles, shapes, motifs, symbols, and patterns. In the three examples shown at bottom, I used the outline of the original spoon handle but created three very different designs to fill the space. For the left-hand design, I used a number of traditional fretted romantic symbols to create a very Welsh type of lovespoon. The middle spoon has a more Continental feel, with a mix of Scandinavian border cuts and a line around the outer edge that I filled with chip carving and a simple initialed heart. The right-hand design is more in the Breton style, with crisp chip carving and an elegant floral design. The result is three radically different designs, all drawn from the same simple root.

Have freewheeling fun with customizing; try anything and everything, and don't be afraid of making something that doesn't work! Your experimentations may not always bear fruit, but even the disasters can teach you valuable lessons that will help improve both your future designing and your carving technique. Make use of tracing paper or photocopiers to copy appealing motifs, shapes, or designs, then further experiment by enlarging and reducing patterns, widening or narrowing stems, bowls, and handles, and trying out a variety of symbols or art styles.

While the intention of this book is not to provide a series of interchangeable and overlayable designs, it *does* provide a comprehensive and rich foundation of the basic styles, shapes, symbols, and patterns essential to developing your own design variations.

The shape and size of a bowl profoundly affects the appearance of the spoon.

Here, three distinct regional styles have been built from the same handle shape.

Guide to Motifs and Symbols

Perhaps the most powerful and recognizable feature of a romantic spoon is its symbolic imagery. Unlike utilitarian or art spoons that only need to function or look beautiful, a true romantic spoon must also make a statement.

While the symbolic imagery found on a Welsh lovespoon is often rich and varied, this wasn't necessarily the case in other areas of Europe. In some places, the only indication of romantic or heartfelt emotion might be a small heart, while in others, the symbolism might be far more subtle and less easily recognizable. It's also important to remember that much of the romantic symbolism now considered "traditional" did not appear in any meaningful way until the twentieth century, many years after the golden age of romantic spoon carving had drawn to a close.

Fretted heart (meaning: love)

Carved heart (meaning: love)

So how can a romantic spoon be discerned from any other spoon? Perhaps the simplest way is to see if there is a **heart** present anywhere in the design. The heart is a universal symbol of love and passion and is found on spoon carvings throughout Europe—but to add a bit of confusion, it may have also appeared as a symbol of religious devotion rather than love. If the heart appeared with a cross, flames, rays (as in rays of light), or pierced by a spear, its meaning was most likely religious rather than romantic, but this occurred only rarely and mostly on Continental spoons originating in Catholic areas. It has been suggested that carved hearts represent greater passion than fretted hearts, as they are more difficult to undertake, but this is unproven and is likely the product of Victorian romanticism.

Another way to spot a romantic spoon is to look for **initials**, **names**, **dates**, or **inscriptions**. Interestingly, these are also something of a rarity that may be explained by lower levels of literacy at the time or, in the case of tester and festival spoons, not having a specific recipient for the spoon in mind. When they do appear on a spoon, it is a clear indication that the piece represented something more than a simple eating utensil.

Mostly, it is the elaborate decoration and lack of signs of wear that indicate an antique spoon was given for romantic rather than utilitarian intent. Spoons that show no food discoloration or even wear were generally displayed rather than used. Frequently, spoons are found in museum collections or at auction that are in pristine condition save for a badly chipped or crudely squared bowl tip. This is usually a sign that a highly prized spoon had at one time or another fallen from its display place on the wall and had been damaged by the resulting collision with a hard stone floor.

It has been suggested that symbols appear in three main types on romantic spoons. There are love symbols such as the aforementioned **hearts** as well as **keys** and **keyholes** (symbolizing the key to one's heart); luck symbols such as **four-leaf clovers** and **wheels of fortune**; and, finally, fertility symbols such as **vines**, **raindrops**, or the **ball-in-cage** motif.

Although it could be argued that symbols of prosperity such as **diamonds** and **vessels of food and drink** fall into the luck category, they are often present on Welsh spoons more as an indication of a man's promise to provide for his wife and family.

European carving, while also featuring the heart symbol prominently, lacked many of the symbols found on Welsh lovespoons. In their place was an emphasis on highly skilled **circular patterns** that expanded on the idea of "the wheel of life"; the circle is said to represent eternity, as it has no beginning or end. These patterns frequently appear from Scandinavia to the Carpathian region in an astonishing variety of forms.

Although there are several traditional symbols still widely in use today, there are no hard-and-fast rules governing what can and can't appear on a romantically carved spoon. Romantic spoons are a statement of passion and are a romantic message from the carver; the symbols found on them should reflect that, whatever appearance they might take. If you have a personal message you want to impart that can be expressed best through a symbol not covered here or traditionally used, you should feel encouraged to include it on your spoon.

Wheel of fortune
(meaning: luck/eternity)

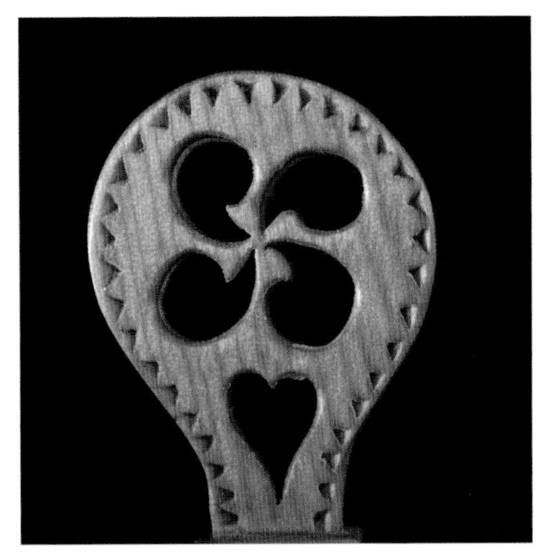

Raindrop
(meaning: fertility/"soul" symbol)

Keyhole
(meaning: security/captured heart)

Ball-in-cage
(meaning: fertility)

Food and drink
(meaning: promise to be a good provider)

Diamonds of prosperity
(meaning: promise to be a good provider)

Wheel with hearts
(meaning: the wheel of life/eternity)

Fretted wheel
(meaning: the wheel of life/eternity)

Pinwheel
(meaning: the wheel of life/eternity)

PART 2

The Patterns

The more than 60 patterns provided in this book span five distinct regions of Northern Europe: Alpine, Brittany, Norway, Sweden, and Wales. The designs are arranged within each section from simplest to most complex and reflect the dominant styles particular to each region. As you explore the various aspects that make each country's spoons identifiable, you can carve the spoons as shown or combine your favorite components into a custom design of your own choosing.

All patterns are given at full size unless otherwise noted.

Alpine

Although the picturesque villages and stunning scenery of the Alpine regions of Europe paint a picture of prosperity and plenty, for many centuries life in the mountains was very difficult, and self-reliance was critical to survival. The men who farmed and forested in these regions became highly skilled woodworkers capable of undertaking everything from framing construction to furniture making and carving. As in other Northern European regions, the long, dark months of winter would be spent mending equipment, maintaining structures, and creating furniture and accoutrements for the household.

Among the objects fashioned during this time would be romantic tokens such as decorated boxes, milking stools, butter-making and baking equipment, and a myriad of farm-related tools. Spoons do not seem to have been made in the profusion they were in other parts of Europe. Those that have survived the centuries appear to have been carved less for initiating relationships and more for use at wedding celebrations or as gifts between family members. Some spoons appear to have been carved by young herders during their summers at pasture; these tend to be more crudely carved and rustic in appearance than the more serious wedding-type spoons.

Alpine spoons are frequently decorated with chip-carved patterning, with many displaying exemplary skill and precise arrangements. The herder-type spoons frequently appear a bit more coarsely carved with patterns that appear to have been laid out freehand rather than with compasses and dividers.

In the mid- to late 1800s and into the early part of the 1900s, a large number of decorative wooden spoons and forks, richly adorned with skillfully carved floral and foliage designs, were made for sale to the tourist trade. Although they are now frequently mistaken for love tokens and have even appeared in literature where they were promoted as "lovespoons," their purpose was decidedly commercial and they had nothing at all to do with courting practices.

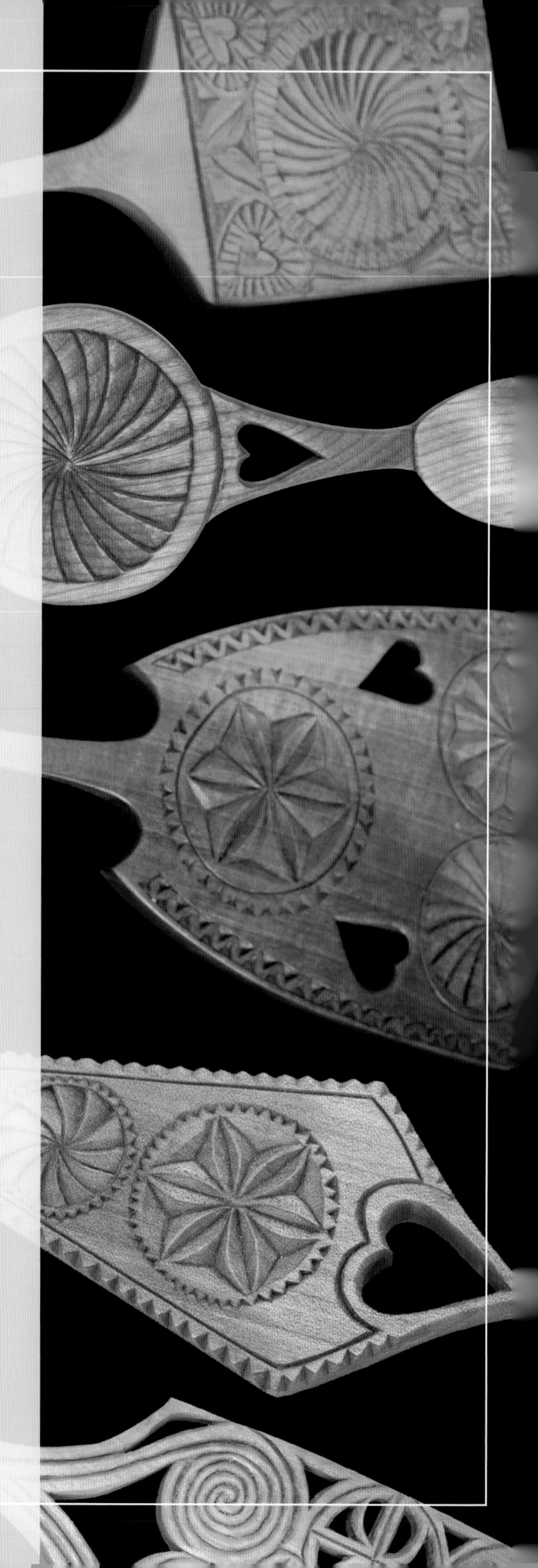

Herder's Spoon

This lovely, simple spoon is a modern adaptation of the type of small, ornamented spoons a herder or field worker might carve for a sweetheart while at pasture. It's easily transportable and requires an absolute minimum of tools to carve.

Chip carving was a popular alpine embellishment on a wide variety of love tokens and both ceremonial and utilitarian woodenware. During the long winter months or time at pasture, young men would use their time to decorate simple pieces of woodwork, transforming them into striking works of folk art.

This little spoon features a pair of common chip-carved motifs: the six-point flower and the pinwheel swirl. You can easily set out both with a basic compass or with a short length of string and a scribing tool, but they were often drawn freehand on more rustic spoons. It is easy to get carried away and cut these types of chip patterns too deep, so begin with shallow cuts. Always cut a pinwheel pattern forward from one segment to the next rather than cutting backward. This will ensure the knife is always heading toward thick uncut stock rather than endangering a thin, already shaped edge.

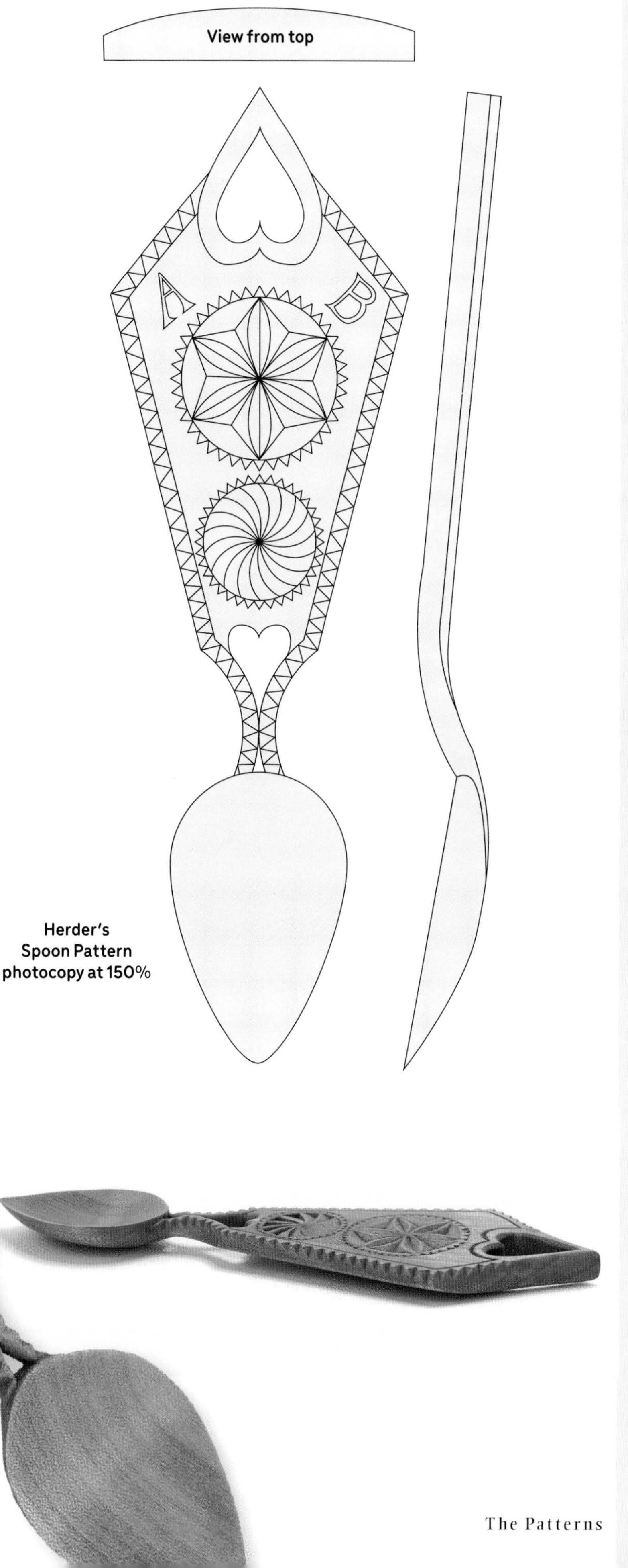

Herder's Spoon Pattern photocopy at 150%

Jewelry Box Panel Spoon

This square panel-style spoon takes its inspiration from the carving found on a highly ornate jewelry box. Larger panel-type spoons tended to feature more fretted work and were slightly more rectangular than this particular example, but this square panel shows off a more freehand style of Alpine chip carving to full effect.

It's best to draw the large and heavily segmented pinwheel with a compass, but with a steady hand you can achieve a close but usually less uniform version. The segments are easy to chip out; use a razor-sharp, straight-bladed knife.

The wonderfully romantic heart details have an elegant, fanlike surrounding detail that can be a bit tricky to carve, so take care not to cut them too deep.

Because the stem is very steeply curved, the safest way to proceed with the carving is to leave it as thick and unworked as possible, only shaping it to its final dimensions when the bowl and handle are both fully carved.

Add an optional chip-carved, repeating diamond pattern along the stem (as in the darker wood example) to bring the design to another level of visual sophistication.

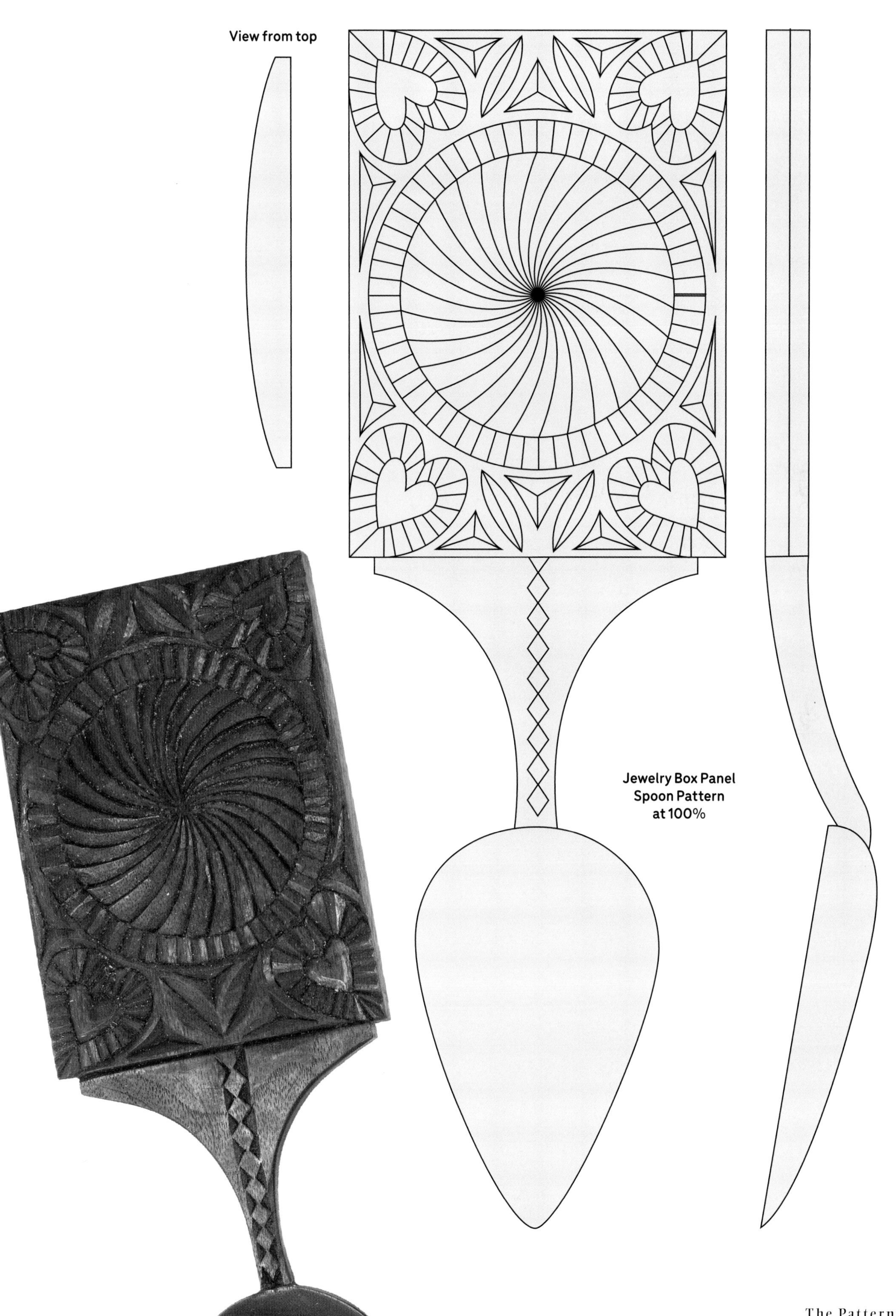
View from top
Jewelry Box Panel
Spoon Pattern
at 100%

Tirolean Courting Spoon

This is a lovely herder's-style spoon of a type that would have been carved by a young man in the high pastures of the Sud Tirol between Austria and Italy. This style would likely date from the latter half of the 1800s and reflects the fondness for fretted "gingerbread" woodwork that swept the world at the time.

The details have a freehand feel to them despite being common, compass-drawn designs. The pattern has a spontaneity and slightly rustic feel that suggests it wasn't carefully plotted out in a workshop, but rather was drawn out as work on the spoon progressed.

The two six-point flowers at the top of the design are very common throughout Europe and are likely used as much for their ease of drawing as they are for the symbolic nature of the circle.

The meaning of the fretted circular patterns in the midsection of the handle are currently unknown, so they could be simply a flight of fancy or they could have symbolic purpose.

Because of the narrowness of the stem and the large fretted cutout at the start of the handle, you should maintain the structural integrity while carving by keeping the stem as thick as possible in this area.

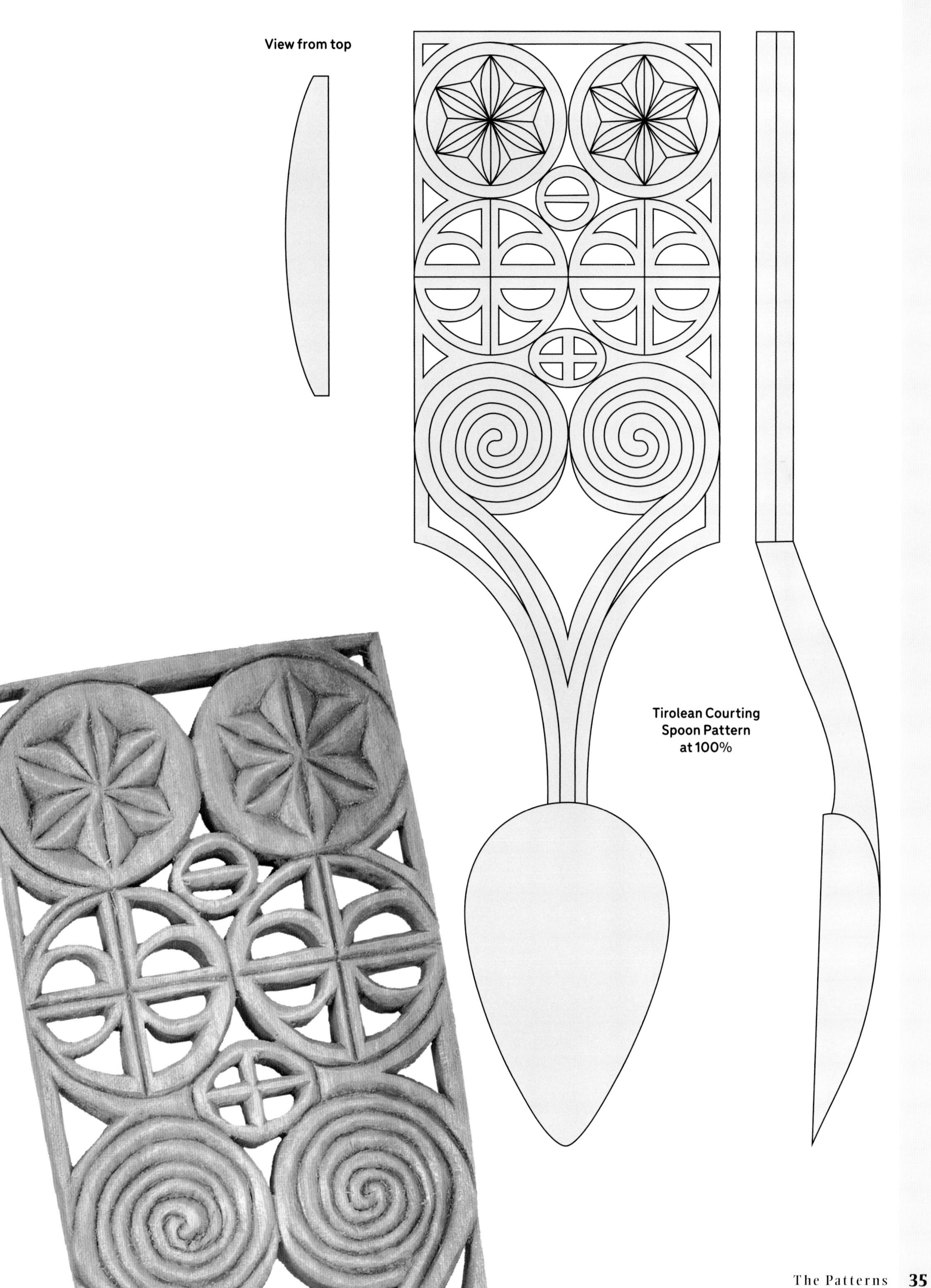
View from top
Tirolean Courting
Spoon Pattern
at 100%

Elegant Panel Spoon

This broad panel spoon is another more modern version of a very traditional style. It is graceful and sophisticated, highlighting crisply organized and rendered Alpine-style chip carving. Although many of the border patterns and the circular motifs are common throughout Northern European woodcarving, they are handled particularly well in the Alpine regions.

The handle has been domed and the back hollowed to create a nice, dynamic "sweep" and to make the spoon more visually appealing. If you leave it flat, it could still look good, but the doming adds another level of drama to the design.

The heart-shaped bowl was not a common feature in Alpine carving, but it looks particularly nice complementing the elegant, curving taper and arched crown of the handle.

The repertoire of flowers, pinwheels, and stars that is possible with compass-drawn circles is enormous, and Alpine carvers were particularly inventive with them. To keep the compass patterns clean and crisp, ensure the front face of the handle has been fully shaped and cleanly finished before committing to any carving. Scraping or sanding this area after the circular patterns have been rendered risks damaging the crisp edges of the carving and ruining the appearance of the pattern.

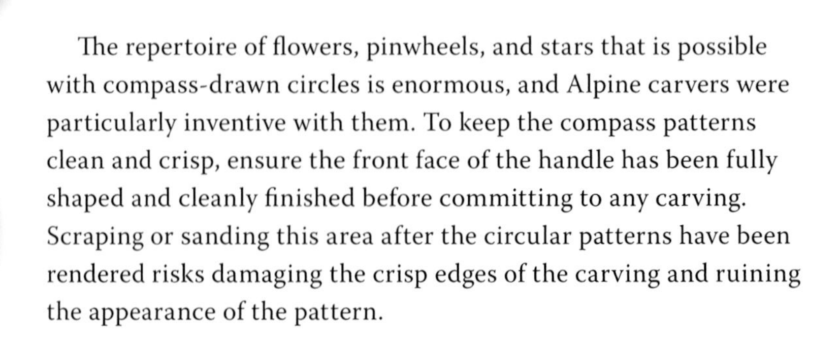

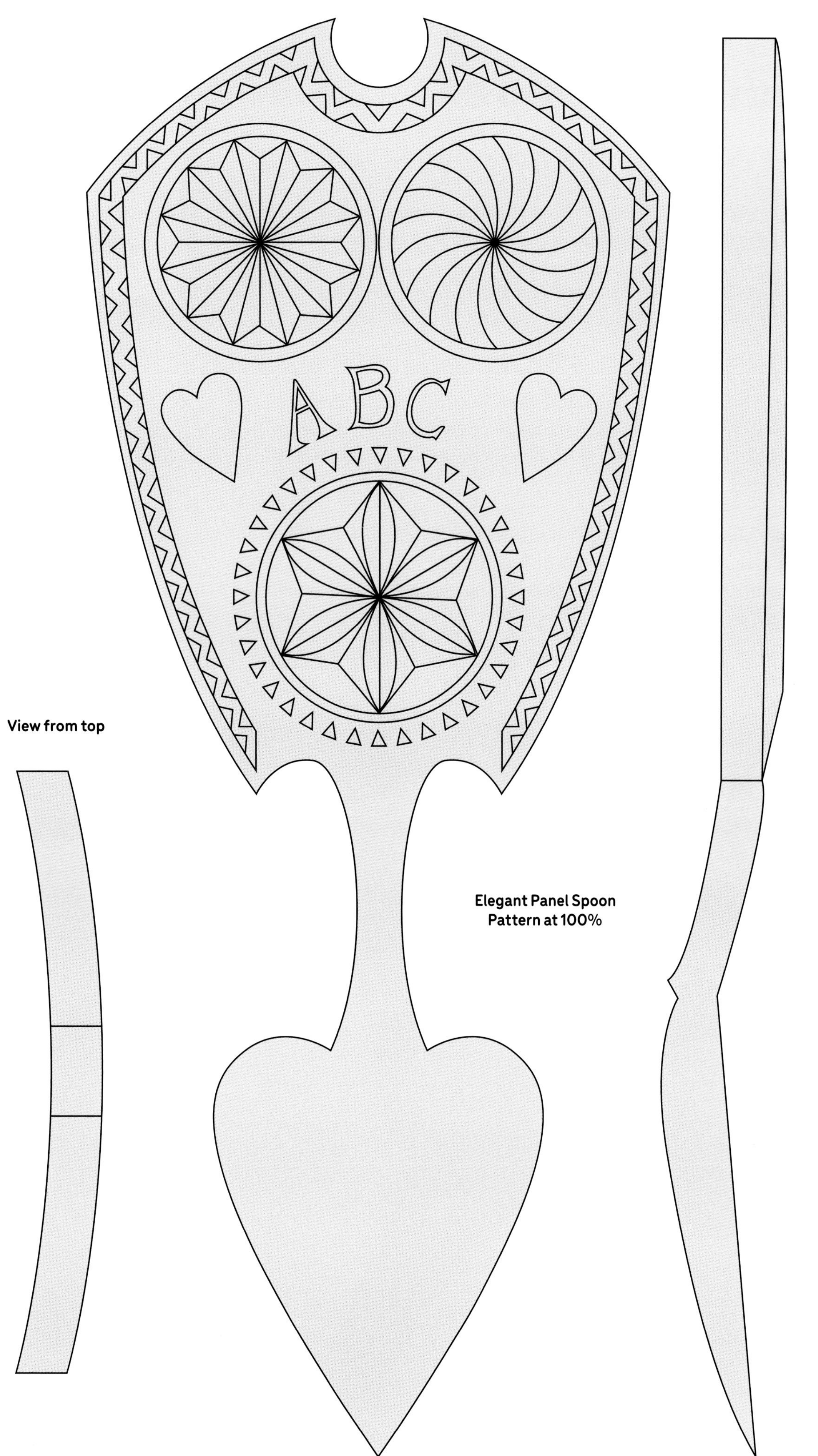

ABC
View from top
Elegant Panel Spoon
Pattern at 100%

Wedding Spoon

This double-ended spoon is of a type that would have been used at a wedding for the couple to share a first meal. Similar to an old Sud Tirolean example, it features an elaborate central pinwheel motif and gracefully sloping stems that culminate in stylish, slightly pointy bowls.

You could further refine the design with the addition of bordering patterns around the pinwheel, but there is something pleasing about the simplicity of this design and the way it complements the cherry wood it has been carved from.

Fully shape and finish the pinwheel section, the bowls, and the front face of the stems before removing any of the back material. Keeping the wood as solid as possible gives support for the front carving and ensures that the stems won't accidentally be snapped from too much downward carving pressure.

The more segmented you make the pinwheel, the more skill you'll need both to lay it out and carve it. The back of the handle, behind the pinwheel, would likely have been left unfinished on antique versions, but on modern spoons it is an ideal place to engrave initials, names, or a wedding date.

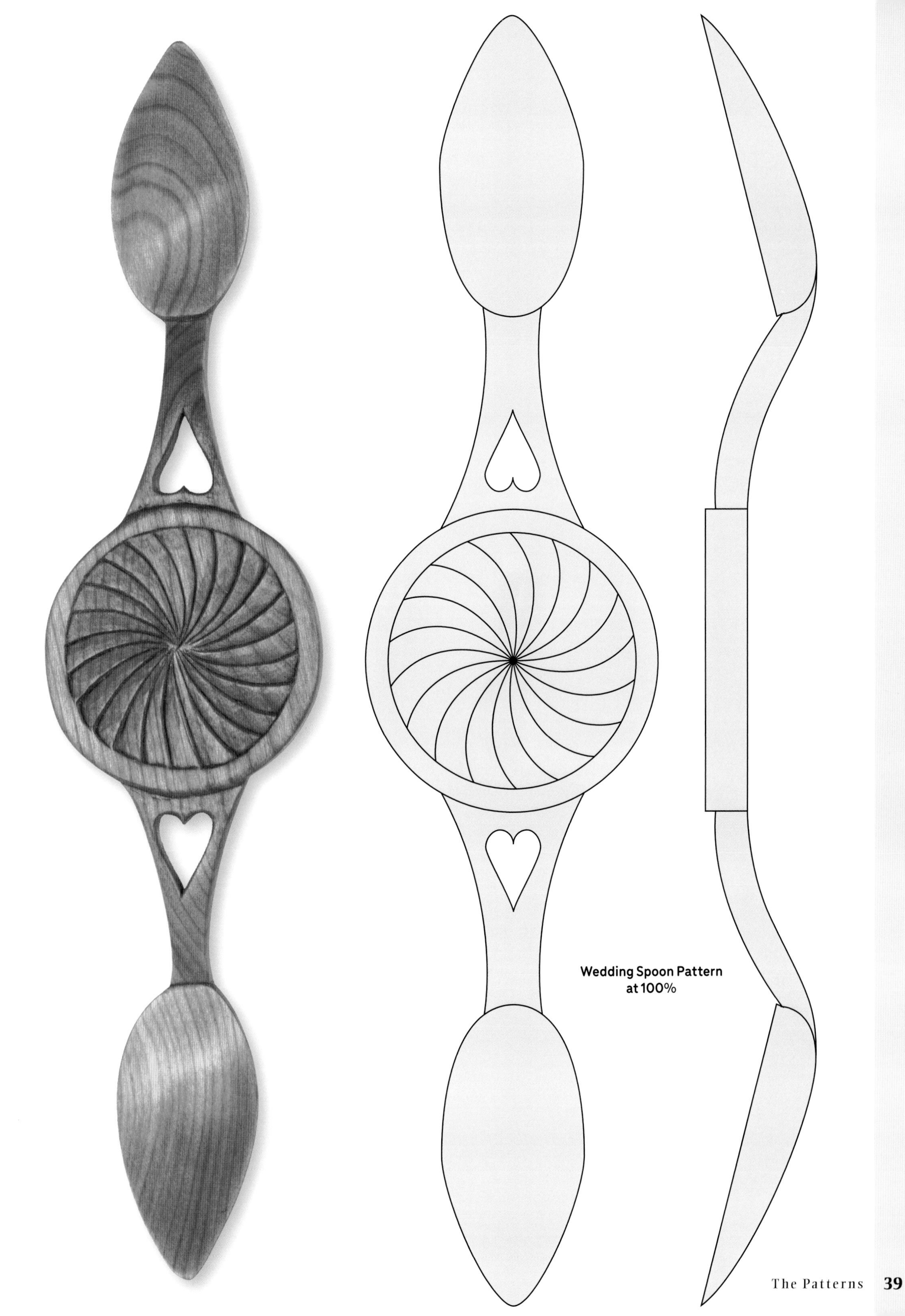
Wedding Spoon Pattern
at 100%

Brittany

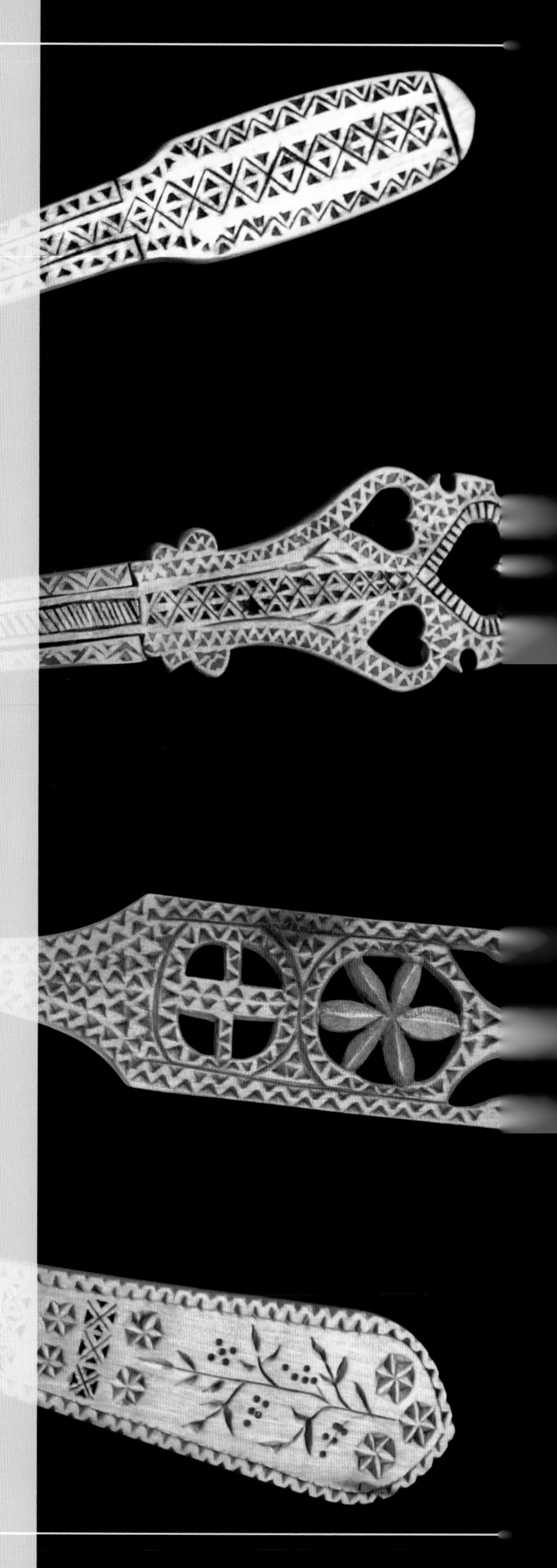

The French region of Brittany's contribution to the romantic spoon tradition is the ornately carved and often inlayed *cuillère de mariage* (wedding spoon). The name is something of a misnomer, however; the description "festival spoon" is probably a more accurate term.

These remarkable and wonderfully elegant spoons differ dramatically from their Continental and Welsh cousins in a number of ways. They are quite unique in their extravagant wax and metal inlays, in the way in which they were used, and in their methods of construction.

While many were presented as tokens of love or courtship initiators by young men to young women, they appear to have been used frequently at festivals, wedding feasts, and celebrations as a way for young men to draw attention to themselves. Often, the spoons would be carved by professionals and would be lavishly decorated with complex geometric chip carvings and inlay work. Many of the best spoons would feature a metal hinge-pin that would allow the spoon to be folded in half for protection and ease of transport. The spoon would be ostentatiously displayed hung from a belt or hatband or from a button on the waistcoat and would be proudly shown off during the celebration. A truly stunning spoon would show one and all that its owner was either a man of substantial talent or that he possessed the financial means to pay for a professional's services. Either way, the goal was to be as impressive as possible to any nearby single young women and their families.

As with most romantic spoon traditions in continental Europe, the making of Breton-style festival spoons has largely died out, but a recent revival of Breton cultural pride has seen renewed interest in the tradition, and several excellent carvers have once again begun carving a variety of *cuillères de mariage* for the tourist and gift markets.

Simple Breton Spoons

When compared to the typically ornate and complex inlaid spoons the Bretons are most famous for, these modest little spoons seem quite subdued. However, the passion of their simple ornamentation indicates a good deal of care has gone into the layout of the designs. Carved with simple chip-carving techniques, these spoons could also be inlayed with various colors of wax for a more dramatic effect.

The first spoon, a simple flower spoon, features a very understated but cleverly carved plant motif composed of an engraved central vine and branches decorated with triangular chip-carved leaves. It's a wonderfully simple yet absolutely evocative piece of folk art. Judging by the handle shape, a spoon design of this type would likely have been based on a metal spoon.

The second spoon, with the heart design, is also a bit reminiscent of a metal spoon, but it has been decorated with a collection of simple freehand motifs. The handle has been gracefully domed and curved, illustrating the type of work a skilled amateur would have performed.

The final spoon, with the fleur-de-lis, is an example of the type of work a keen amateur (bordering on professional) would have undertaken. The six-point flower, fleur-de-lis, and more intricate chip carving indicate a greater level of technical skill and design awareness. This particular type of spoon could have either been given as a love token or used to show off at festivals and gatherings.

A sharp straight knife with a fine tip is extremely useful for ensuring that you cut the delicate chip carving as cleanly as possible. Although these are straightforward and relatively basic designs, crisp cuts are essential to avoid ragged edges and a murky appearance. Shape any doming or arching into the top face of the handle before committing to the chip carving.

Simple Breton Spoons Pattern
at 100%

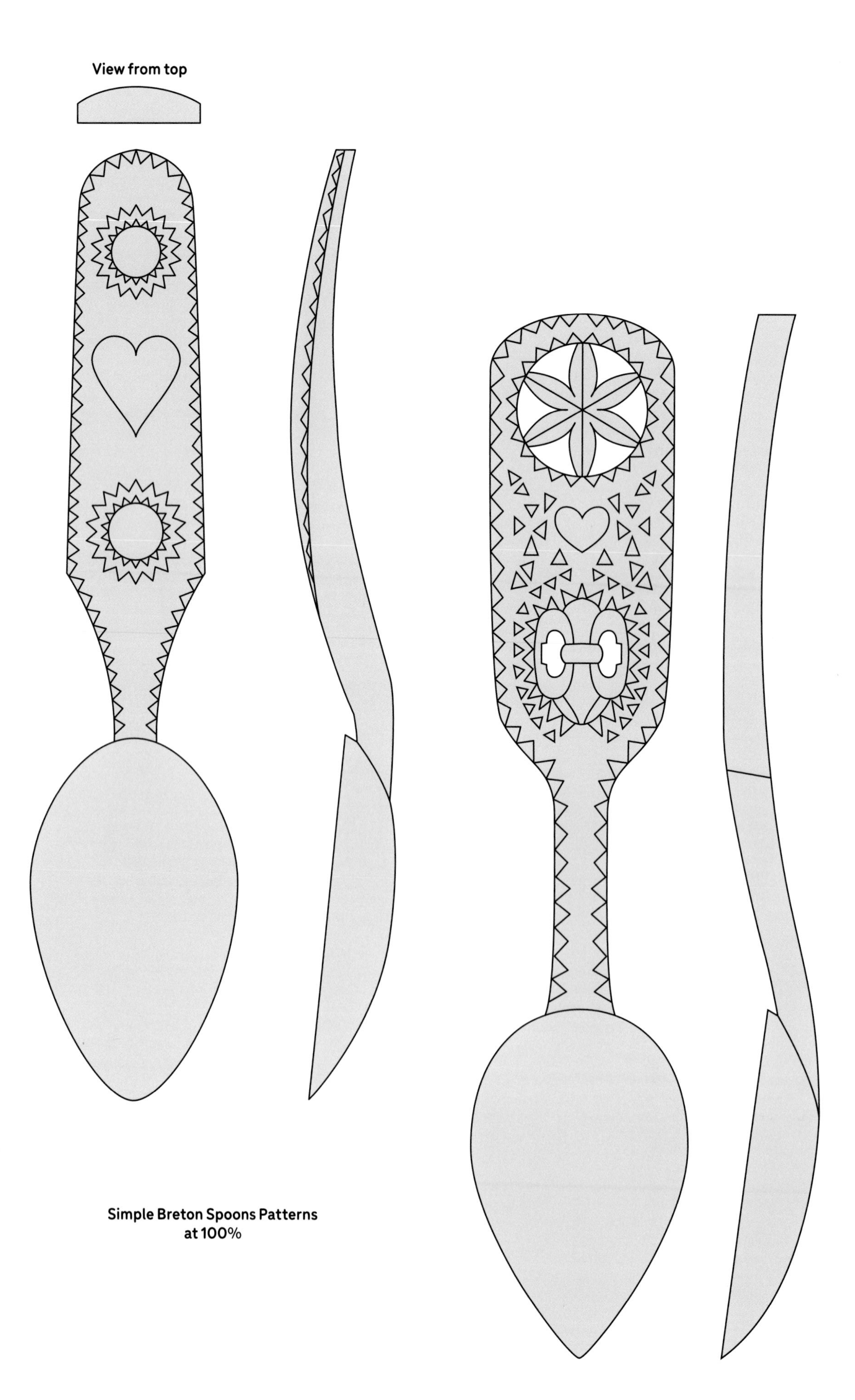

Simple Breton Spoons Patterns
at 100%

Breton Flowers Spoon

This simple design has been produced three different ways to illustrate the differences that slight variations in carving technique make to a design. The first spoon has had the foliage section of the design engraved by chip carving; the middle spoon has had the foliage carved in low relief; and the third spoon has been etched and inlaid with sealing wax.

The spoon is notable for its wide stem, gentle taper, and thinness. Although fairly broad through the stem, the continuation of the taper makes the spoon appear lighter and more balanced than it would if the sides of the handle were square to each other. A further chamfer cut near the bowl creates an illusion the stem is narrower than it actually is.

Undertake the subtle border detail with the sharpest possible knife to keep the edges of the cuts crisp and to avoid chipping the herringbone detail.

Sealing wax inlay was an extremely popular material with Breton carvers and was used with great dexterity and flair. Even the simplest splashes of color (such as the red berries here, which are simple drilled holes filled with wax) can substantially enliven a design.

Breton Flowers Spoon Pattern at 100%

Breton Geometric Pattern Spoon

This simple, yet highly effective design has been rendered in a variety of ways to illustrate how even the subtlest of alterations can have a profound effect on the finished spoon.

To achieve its appearance of apparent complexity, the design relies on the repetition of simple chip-carved triangles arranged along a series of straight lines. Repetition of simple forms was often used by romantic spoon carvers throughout Europe to exaggerate the intricacy of their designs and is also a useful way for beginner carvers to become more adept at both carving and design.

Get comfortable with inlaying a single color before attempting a multicolored pattern. When inlaying multiple colors, carve and wax each particular section by color rather than cutting out the whole design at once. This reduces the chances of wax getting into the wrong areas. Plot with colored pencils before committing to carving. Remove excess wax with a sharp, flat chisel or cabinet scraper. Never use abrasive papers, as they create heat and friction that scratches the smooth surface of the wax and risks smearing the softened wax into undesired areas.

This is a design that looks great on a generously curved handle and is also equally impressive without inlay. Leave the back solid for as long as possible to ensure support while chip carving the front, as excessive downward pressure on a curved handle is a recipe for disaster. As with all chip carving, use a razor-sharp blade to keep the cuts neat and uniform and guard against unwanted fuzzing of the edges that can draw in wax and leave a sloppy-looking pattern.

Breton Geometric Pattern
Spoon Pattern
at 100%

Breton Six-Point Star Spoon

This wonderful design has the exuberant but slightly rustic feel of a work created by a talented amateur, but its careful arrangement, lovely chip patterns, and lack of romantic symbolism are also typical of the type of work carried out by professional carvers.

The most ornately carved of the Breton spoons were invariably crafted from dense, homogenous material such as boxwood and apple wood. These types of timbers allowed carvers to cleanly render the intense chip-carved patterns common to Breton design. Few Breton spoons were carved from dark timbers or stained dark colors, as darker woods tend to disguise, rather than highlight, the intricate geometric chip-carved decorations.

Although the central circular patterns here have been drawn freehand and lack the precision of compass-drawn designs, they possess a liveliness that can sometimes be lost with meticulous uniformity.

This spoon has a gently domed back surface on the handle to lend the fragile design some extra support. The back of the stem has also been left a bit thick to support the junction between it and the tilted bowl.

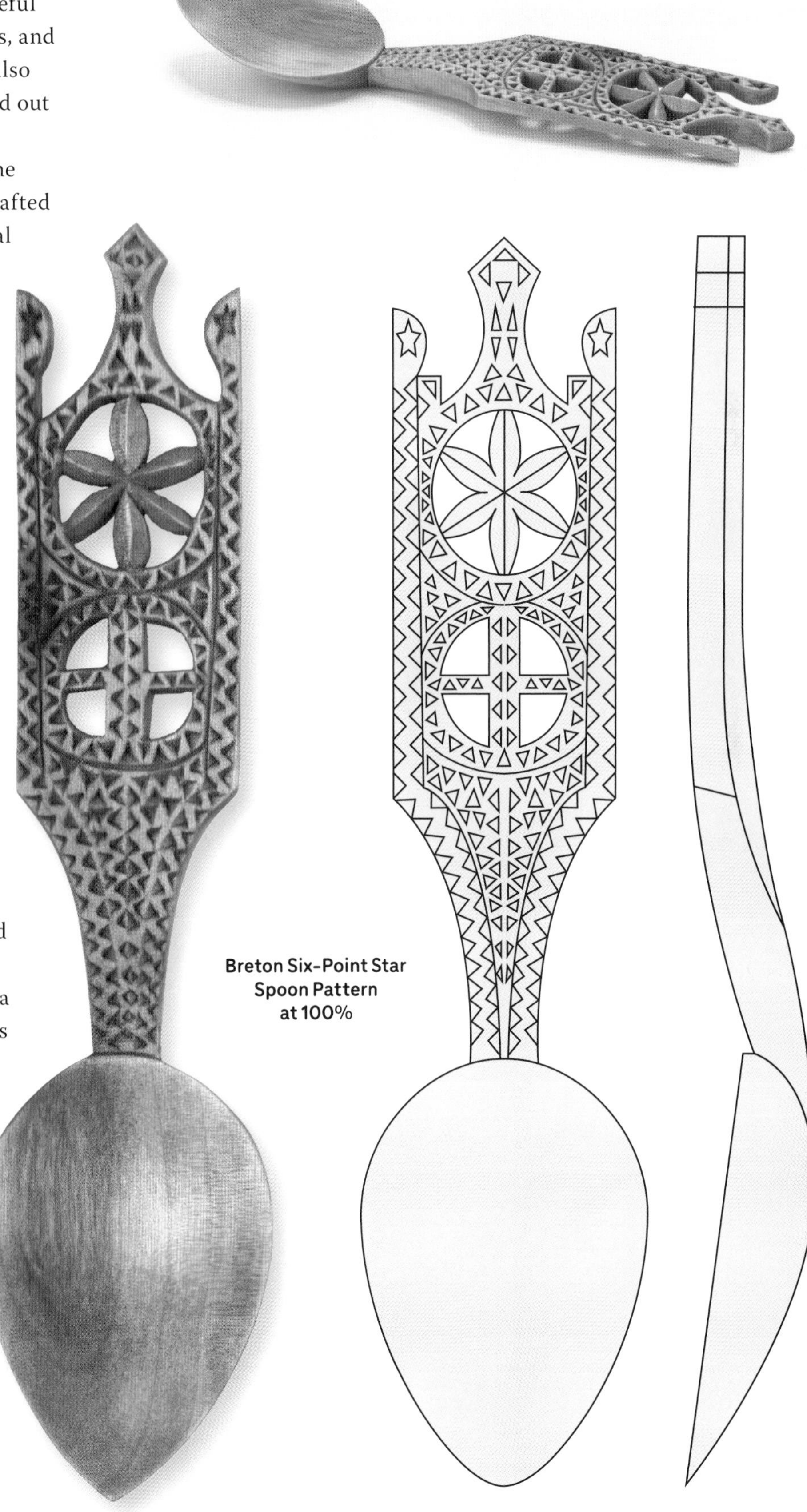

Breton Six-Point Star Spoon Pattern at 100%

Folding Spoon

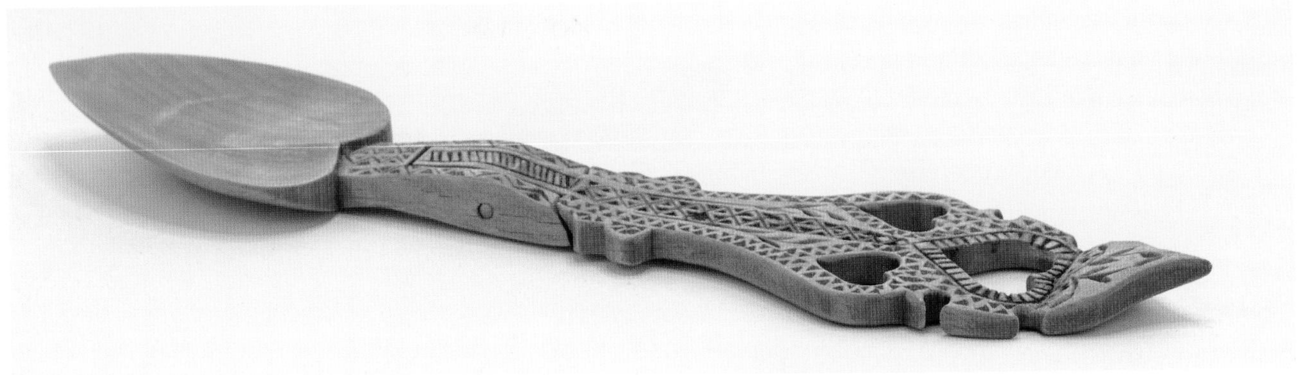

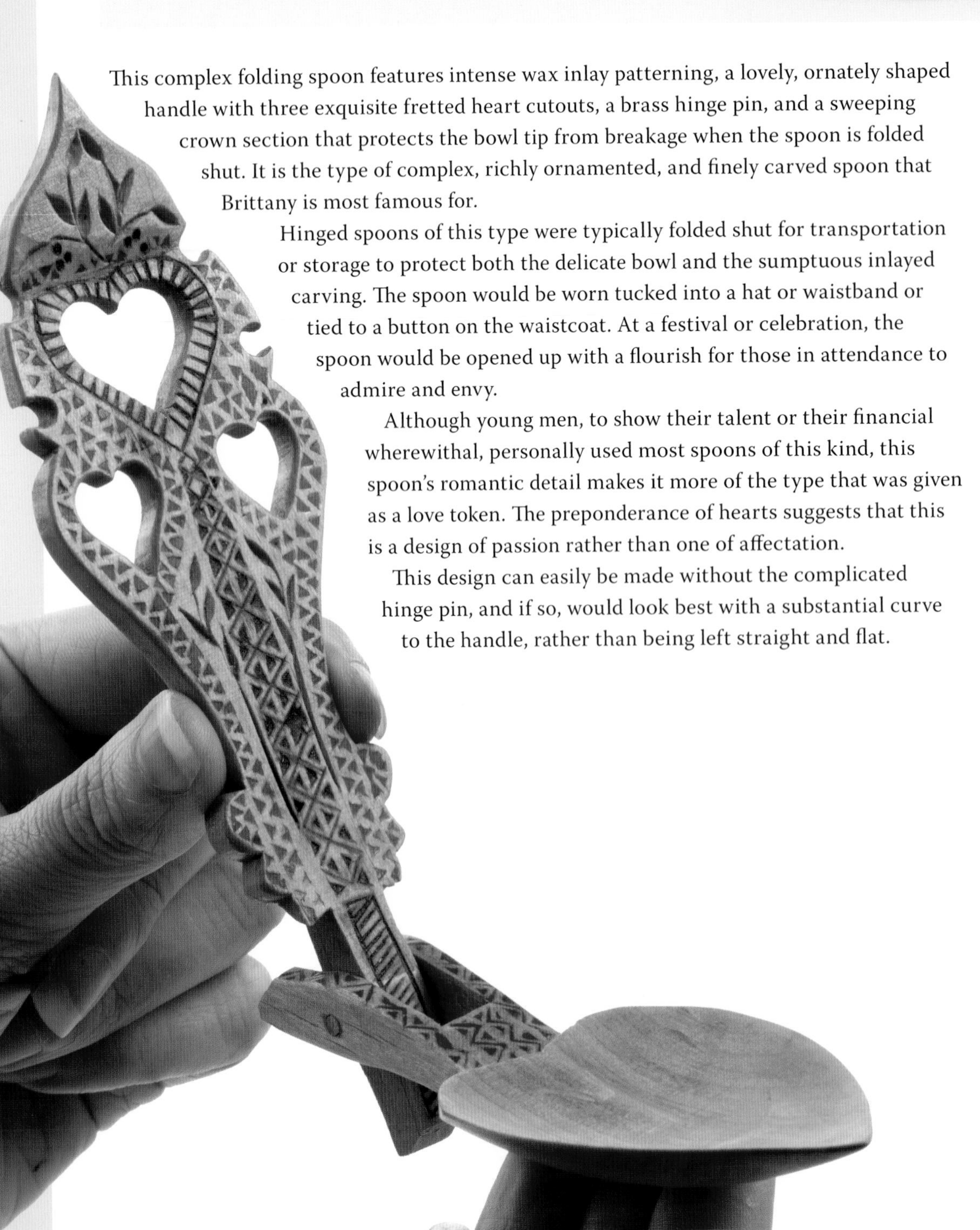

This complex folding spoon features intense wax inlay patterning, a lovely, ornately shaped handle with three exquisite fretted heart cutouts, a brass hinge pin, and a sweeping crown section that protects the bowl tip from breakage when the spoon is folded shut. It is the type of complex, richly ornamented, and finely carved spoon that Brittany is most famous for.

Hinged spoons of this type were typically folded shut for transportation or storage to protect both the delicate bowl and the sumptuous inlayed carving. The spoon would be worn tucked into a hat or waistband or tied to a button on the waistcoat. At a festival or celebration, the spoon would be opened up with a flourish for those in attendance to admire and envy.

Although young men, to show their talent or their financial wherewithal, personally used most spoons of this kind, this spoon's romantic detail makes it more of the type that was given as a love token. The preponderance of hearts suggests that this is a design of passion rather than one of affectation.

This design can easily be made without the complicated hinge pin, and if so, would look best with a substantial curve to the handle, rather than being left straight and flat.

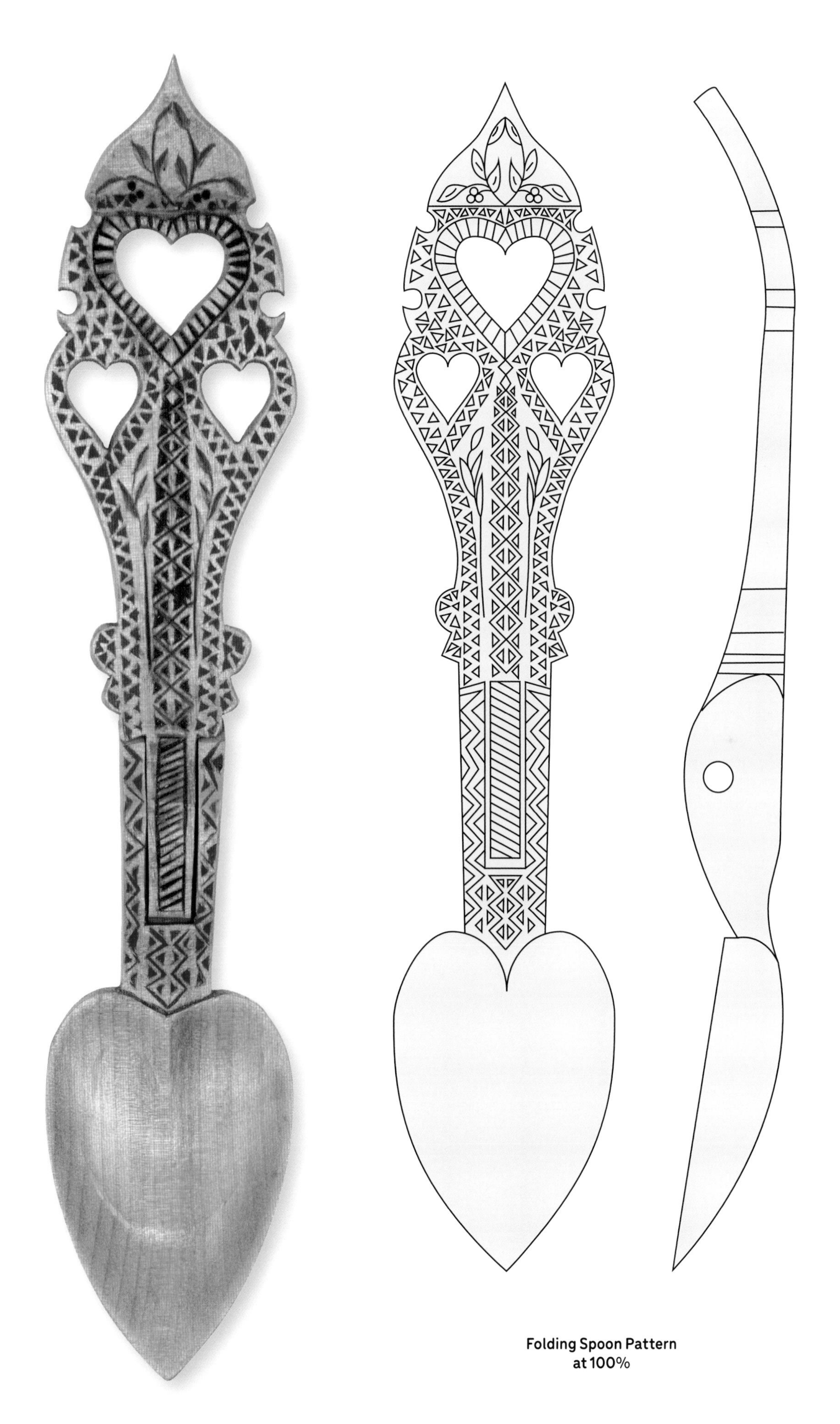

Folding Spoon Pattern
at 100%

Norway

The Norwegians are justifiably renowned for their prodigious woodworking skills and are rightly very proud of their wood traditions. Norway has a rich custom of romantic spoon carving that rivals neighboring Sweden's and dates back to at least the early 1700s. Despite the fact that Norwegian carvers created a number of intriguing romantic, utilitarian, and commercial spoon styles, today the best known of the Norwegian romantic spoons is the double-handled, chain-linked wedding spoon. Although romantic spoon carving has now largely died out in Norway, there is a small but tenacious demand for these classic wedding spoons, and couples both in Norway and abroad are once again making them a part of their wedding ceremonies.

There is, however, much more to Norwegian spoon tradition than just wedding spoons. Spectacular acanthus-leaf-handled spoons were professionally carved for the gift and tourist market, elegant courting spoons were carved by young men for their lady loves, and still other spoons were carved and sold through a network of government-sponsored retail agents. These shops, called *Husfliden*, fostered national pride in traditional woodcraft, and many professionals and dedicated amateurs would spend the winter months carving spoons that they would sell through these government retailers in the spring and summer.

As with other regions, the spoons carved by professionals and serious amateurs are of extremely high quality, with impeccable craftsmanship, crisp design, and excellent finishing. The spoons of amorous amateurs are often more rustic and coarsely carved, but even they display the highly developed level of technical ability and good design sense that is common to those well versed and comfortable working in wood.

The Norwegians, like their Swedish neighbors, often decorated their spoon bowls with elaborate kolrosing patterns that they colored with coal dust or coffee grounds. These lovely etched designs may have been maker's marks among the professional carvers, but on most spoons they appear to be spontaneous freehand creations.

Birch was the wood of choice for most Norwegian carvers; its creamy, homogenous grain and soft, pale tone are ideally suited for spoon carving, and it takes both carved and etched decoration beautifully.

Notched Handle Spoon

Of the type likely inspired by metal spoon designs, this straightforward spoon shows graceful, thoughtful Norwegian spoon carving at its best. The design is basic but well considered, with a dynamic flow to the taper of the handle, perfectly placed and very restrained fretted decoration, and an elegant, slightly pointed bowl. The handle has also been stylishly domed and the edges softened to make the spoon both a tactile and visual pleasure. The darker spoon is spalted birch and the lighter is maple; since the handle is mostly unadorned, this is a wonderful design for showing the attractive wood grain and figure to its maximum potential.

You must treat the notches on the sides of the handle deftly. If the two sides are even slightly out of alignment, the spoon will lose its balance and elegance and become clumsy. Make sure the notches are very cleanly cut and that the depth of the cut matches on both sides.

Make the fretted heart large enough to be noticeable, but not big enough to become overwhelming. Center it perfectly to avoid throwing the design out of balance. Leave the stem of the handle as thick as possible until all other work is completed in order to limit unfortunate accidents.

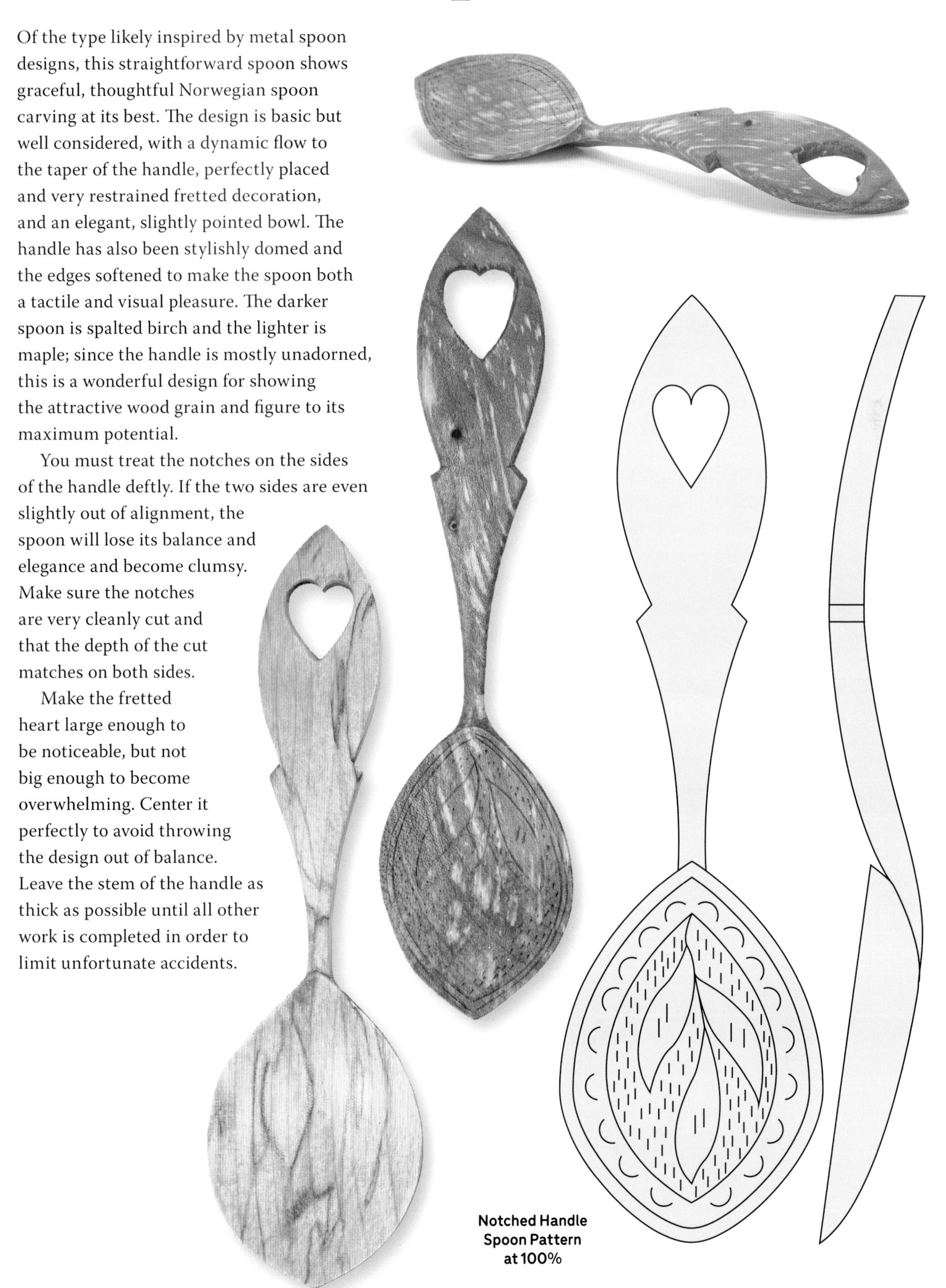

Notched Handle Spoon Pattern at 100%

Double Hearts Spoon

This charming, straightforward stacked heart design repeats a motif that was popular throughout Scandinavia; a number of similar spoons are held in several Norwegian and Swedish museums. The hearts most certainly suggest a sentimental intent to the spoon, but whether it was a romantic love token or the type of gift given by a father to a child is unknown.

The very basic design is greatly enhanced by the addition of a simple line surrounding each fretted heart. Take care; it can be difficult to render a line like this cleanly and precisely because the wood grain changes direction several times, so the scribed line can easily wander if you are not being attentive.

The kolrosed pattern in the bowl (so called because, in the old days, the lines would be scribed and then packed with coal dust to darken them) further decorates a simple design and may have been something of a carver's mark.

Although this spoon would look good carved from flat material, working a generous curve into both handle and stem will give the simple spoon more life and considerably more sophistication.

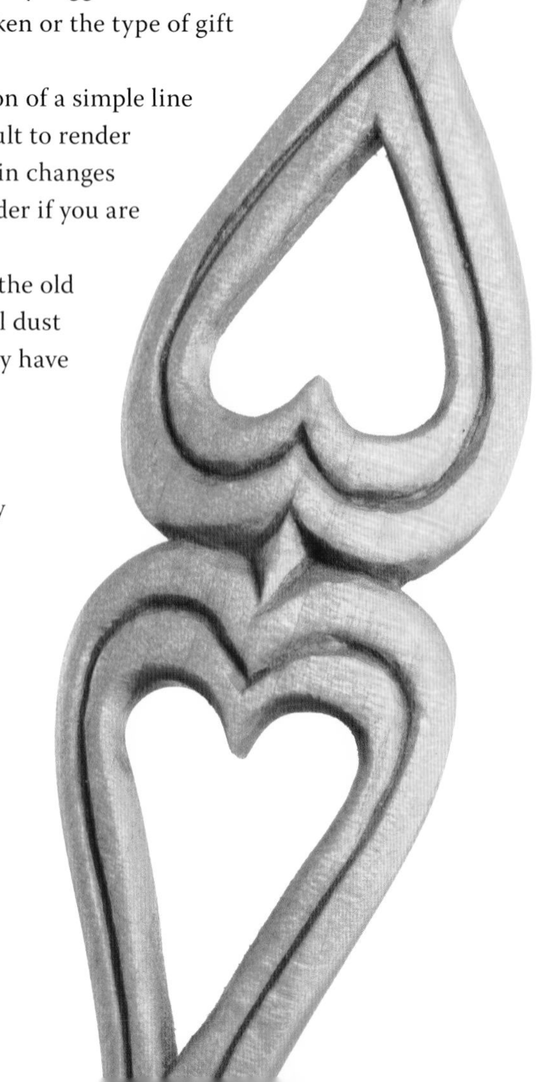

Double Hearts Spoon Pattern at 100%

Stylized Hearts Spoon

A spoon with a design like this was likely a courting gift, as it is romantic, well considered, and carefully crafted. The seemingly undemanding design is actually far more complex than appears at first glance. The fretted hearts are exceptionally well balanced, drawing the eye along the spoon handle while not being so repetitious as to become tedious. They are cleanly fretted with gently rounded edges that lend them a softer appearance. This softness is echoed by the gracefully domed handle, with its lightly smoothed edges.

The oval bowl has been slightly elongated to echo the flow of the handle and is slightly tilted from its tip toward its stem. The junction between the stem and the handle has been kept fairly robust, so despite the lacelike fretting, the spoon is surprisingly sturdy.

Make sure the handle is fully domed and finished before undertaking the chip carving. This will ensure that the chip-carved details remain crisp and are not damaged by cutting, sanding, or scraping. Carefully finish the side edges and the back of the handle, leaving no rough spots or unevenness.

Stylized Hearts Spoon Pattern
at 100%

Four Hearts Spoon

Four hearts arranged tip to tip in a cross or circle is a popular motif in Scandinavian spoon design. This arrangement appears in a wide variety of ways in both Norway and Sweden. These two versions of the same design illustrate the difference the addition of some simple chip-carved bordering can make to the design.

Traditionally, the hearts would have been fretted using the tip of a straight knife, as it was only in later years that jeweler's saws and scroll saws became available and popular. The freehand nature of fretting with a straight knife meant that many times the hearts would not come out particularly uniform, and, often, the little tip at the center of the heart's crown would be left more pronounced and rounded than it appears on modern spoons.

Because the stem is quite narrow on this spoon, a good amount of stock thickness has been left to offer the area adequate support. Although a flat-faced handle would look nice, both of these versions have been given a domed face to add some visual appeal. You can decorate the bowl with kolrosing or, if the grain is particularly attractive, leave it unornamented as shown here.

Four Hearts Spoon Pattern at 100%

Fan Spoon

This spoon amply illustrates the type of high-quality design and workmanship Norwegian woodcarvers are famous for. With its elegant crown detail and lovely heart detail mid-handle, it is likely a spoon like this would have been carved as a love token. It may have been proudly displayed in a spoon rack where both its craftsmanship and the desirability of the young woman who owned it could be appreciated by family and visitors.

The stylish fan detail at the crown requires careful carving with a sharp straight knife to ensure crisp detailing and clean edges. Lines that aren't fair or that vary in depth and width will ruin the fan's graceful flow and make the carving look ungainly.

The heart element is another tricky detail to carve. The heart is slightly raised from the circular backing; carve it precisely to maintain its bright appearance. Wandering lines or fuzzy edges will make the carving look murky and amateurish.

The stem of this spoon is extremely fine and is a constant risk for breakage. The spoon bowl is raised slightly higher than is typical on most spoons, which helps it to stand out visually. Take care that you don't chip the fragile edge of the bowl with errant cuts when shaping the stem.

Kolrosing the bowl works particularly well with this design; the crown is visually busy, but the long and subdued stem allows a more "active" bowl to balance the design.

Fan Spoon Pattern at 100%

Spoon Rack Display Spoon

This is another charming romantic spoon of the sort likely intended as a courtship gift and which probably would have been displayed in a spoon rack or dowry chest. Despite its straightforward and somewhat minimal handle, the spoon displays both a great deal of craftsmanship and a crisp design.

The handle has been left slightly thicker than would be expected on a light little design like this, making the spoon much more robust than it appears. At the center of the handle, the circular section that features an attractive relief-carved stylized floral pattern also acts to break up the monotony of an uninterrupted taper along the handle. It is a simple feature, but one that adds a remarkable visual appeal to an otherwise ordinary handle.

Lay out the chip carving precisely and carefully in order to achieve a pleasing and organized design, which ultimately looks far more complex than it is. As with all chip-carved patterns, make sure to maintain consistency; keep the depth and width of each cut uniform.

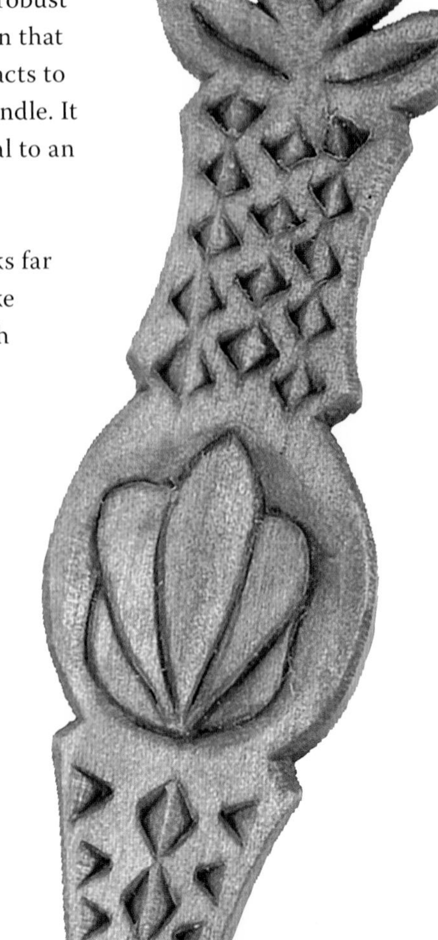

Spoon Rack Display Spoon Pattern at 100%

Floral Heart Spoon

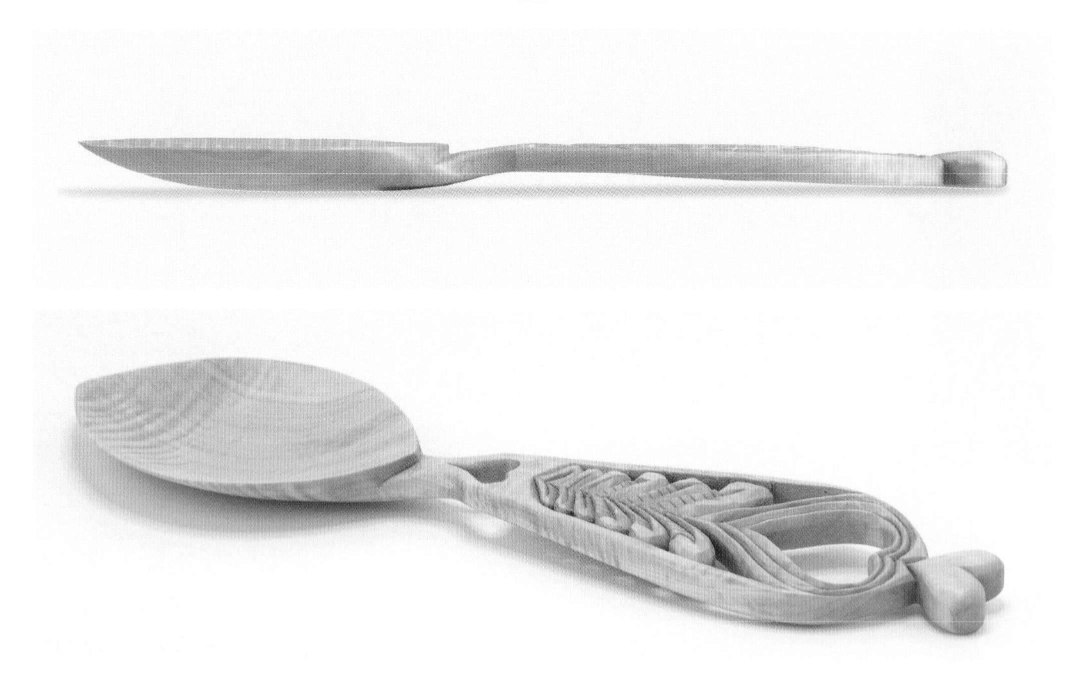

This spoon requires a deft hand to carve. When rendering the linework surrounding the large fretted heart, take care to create a consistent depth and width while being conscious of the vagaries of the wood's grain. You'll also need a very sharp knife for carving the stylized foliage pattern mid-handle. Inadvertent chip-outs are always possible when repeatedly cutting cross-grain, as is required with this pattern. Fraying and tearing of the grain is a possibility if the knife's blade isn't kept in top condition.

While most Norwegian spoons of this type would have featured kolrosing etched into the bowl, this example has been left unadorned to highlight the wood's stunning tiger-stripe figure. The bowl is also notable for its unique oval shape with points at either end.

Generously round over the edges on the little heart at the crown to greatly enhance it. Judicious rounding will also help soften the foliage detail and give it a much more tactile appearance than it would have if left with square edges.

The fretted detail near the stem means that this spoon suffers from a weakening of structural support in the area. You can only overcome this by adding some thickness to the back of the stem or by exercising great caution during carving.

Floral Heart Spoon Pattern at 100%

Acanthus Spoon

Acanthus leaf spoons were typically carved more for the retail and tourist trades than as romantic tokens. However, this one is included because acanthus is an enjoyable challenge to carve and can be used in a variety of ways to enhance carvings and romantic designs. Many of the acanthus spoons found in museums and private collections are staggeringly complex, beautifully and immaculately carved, and feature designs that utilize several layers twisted around one another. Most, if not all, of these spoons would have been professionally carved and expensive to purchase, so they were not typically the spoons of lovestruck amateur carvers.

This modest design is representative of a good-quality, basic design that could be carved by an enthusiastic beginner. It offers an excellent lesson in some of the basic skills required for this type of carving, such as layout, shaping, and engraving.

Choose a lighter-toned wood for this design to allow the detailing of the acanthus to be more visible, especially in the areas where shallow lines define and separate the leaves. The spoon has a fairly large bowl; keep the bowl simple so that it does not clash with the busy appearance of the handle. Save carving the narrow stem until you reach the end of the project. Shaping a slight dome or double angle into the face of the handle before detailing the acanthus leaves will help to make the flow of the leaves more natural and believable.

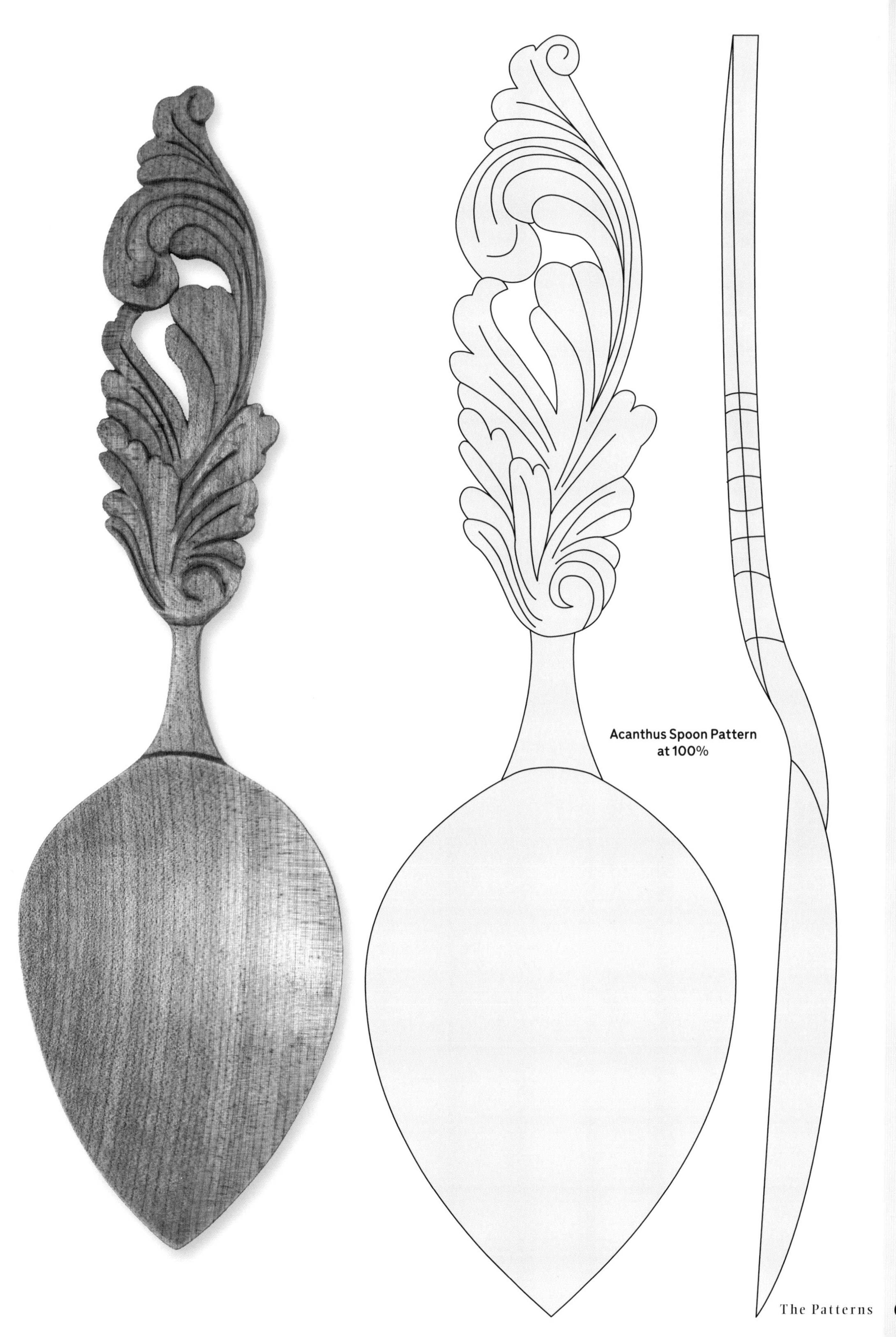
Acanthus Spoon Pattern
at 100%

Wedding Blocks Spoon

This small spoon is of a type that may well have been given as a wedding gift; its pair of neatly carved pyramidal blocks at the crown hints at the notion of two joined together, as in matrimony.

Although the spoon looks relatively straightforward, it must be carved from a fairly thick piece of wood to accommodate the linked blocks. The blocks themselves are square at their tops with equal widths and depths, a measurement dictated by the thickness of the available timber.

As with most Norwegian and Swedish spoons, this design features a fairly pronounced sweep through the handle and stem. Leave the material in this section until the spoon is almost complete, only removing it at the very end. Shape and detail the blocks before they are separated from the handle, leaving the blocks and handle rings as substantial as possible for as long as possible.

You can further embellish the unfinished section at the top of the handle with the addition of initials, names, or dates. It would also look particularly attractive with a large pinwheel circle or fretted pattern.

Wedding Blocks Spoon Pattern at 100%

Chain Wedding Spoons

These are the famous Norwegian wedding spoons, carved in great numbers from the 1800s. Sometimes families became known for their spoon carving, with skills being passed from generation to generation. These spoons are still popular to this day, and carvers continue to craft them following the traditional form.

Although wedding spoon lore proposes that the entire set, including the chain, be carved from a single timber, it is more likely that in all but exceptional cases, the spoons were made in three pieces. It would require a good deal more lumber, time, and care to make a set from a single board, so it is unlikely that professionals would wish to waste their time and material in this way.

While the handles are fairly straightforward to carve, they do offer a couple of interesting challenges. You will need very sharp small gouges to carve the unique little faces at the center of the crowns in order to cut them really cleanly. Carve the little animal faces on the top corners of the handles to be as close to three-dimensional as possible, and make sure the engraving that follows the fretted pattern through the handle does not get too deep or wide.

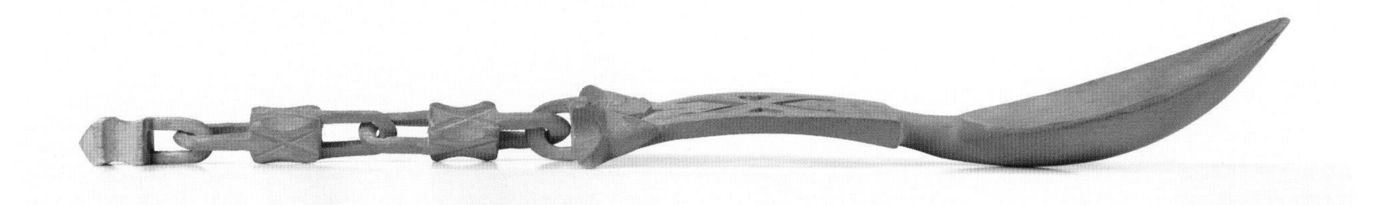

The chain links will present most of the technical challenges when carving a set of these wedding spoons. These links differ from the typical chain link that most carvers are familiar with in that each segment features a rectangular section of solid wood that is usually decorated with an engraved X and a deep V-shaped cut at each edge of the link. The key to successfully cutting Norwegian-style links is to carefully lay out the links on a length of ½ inch (1.3cm) by ½ inch (1.3cm) timber (a 17-inch [43cm] length is usually plenty) before committing to any cutting. Saw and clear the marked-out areas to reveal the rectangular solid blocks, then engrave an X on each face of the block before cutting the corner Vs. With the blocks all cut, begin clearing a cross-shaped section between each block that will be shaped into the two halves of the link. Use a fine straight knife to cut this area and to separate the links. With the links separated, spend some time to clean up each link with the straight knife. To join the chain to the handles, very carefully split the end links and slide the handle's crown loop into the link. Use carpenter's yellow glue or cyanoacrylate glue to glue the link back together, and then carefully carve the area to disguise the join.

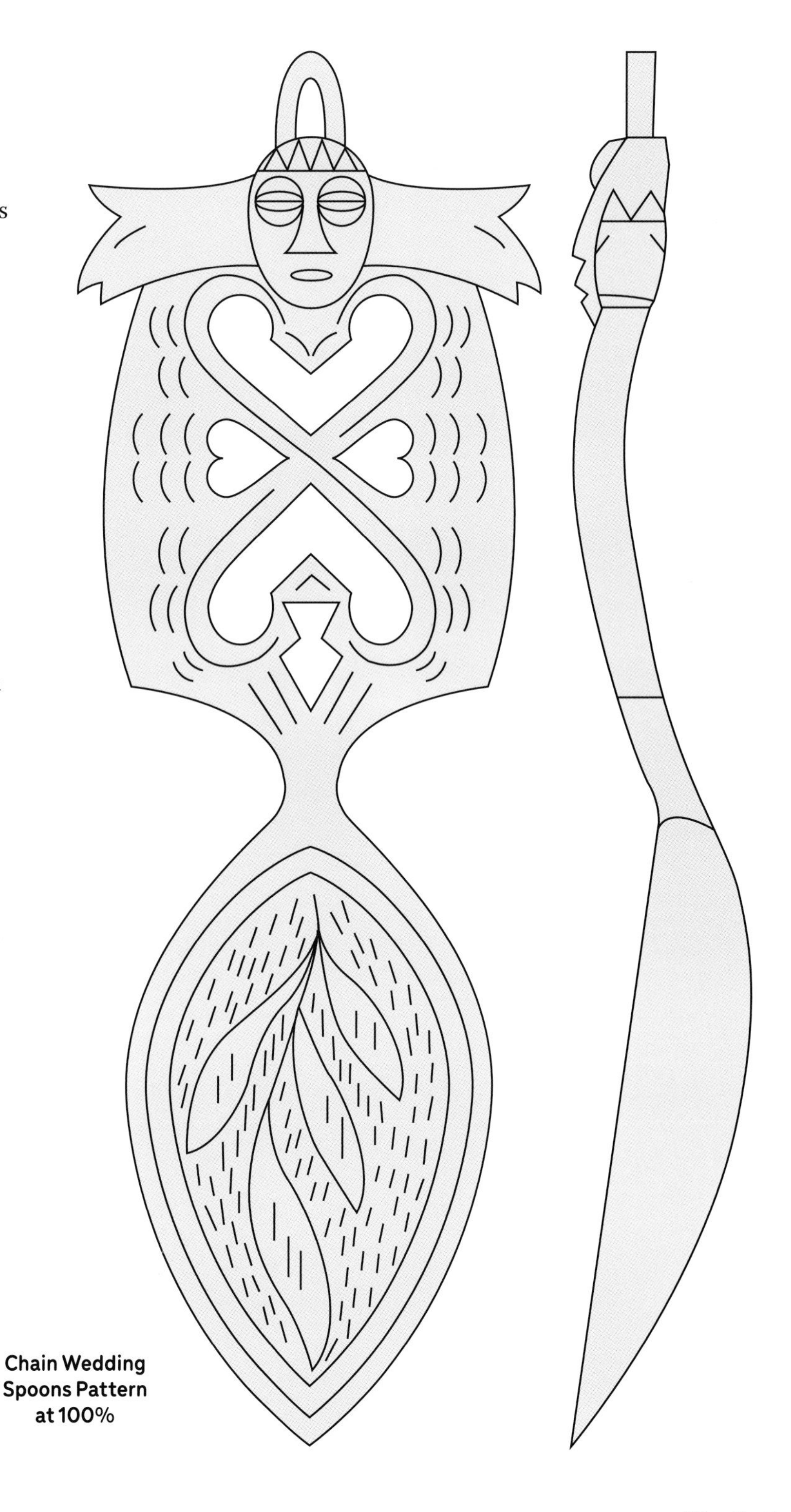

Chain Wedding Spoons Pattern at 100%

Sweden

Although the Welsh lovespoon is the best known of the romantic spoons, it could be argued the Swedish tradition is every bit as rich and possibly more complex. While most Swedish romantic spoons tended be more conservative in design than their Welsh counterparts, their craftsmanship was exemplary and their range of purpose much more extensive. Whereas Welsh lovespoons were primarily a gift given to initiate a serious courtship, Swedish spoons could be given for a variety of purposes ranging from simple "testing the waters"–type spoons through to marital spoons used to help cement the union on the big day.

In some regions, spoons were given to initiate courtships; in others, they were a much more serious endeavor in line with a betrothal gift. In still other places, young men would give away a number of simply designed and carved spoons and would gauge the receptions their gifts elicited from the young women who received them. Future attention could thus be focused where there had been a more positive response. In more conservative areas, this sort of pre-engagement gift giving was frowned upon and was considered unseemly behavior. Thus, young girls who collected many spoons might be viewed as ultra-desirable in one region but be thought to have questionable morals in another.

In certain regions, the young man gave more modest gifts at courtship, with elaborately crafted items such as ornate spoons forming part of a bridal token given when an engagement was announced.

Finally, in a few areas, spoons would not be given until the wedding, where they were used as a way of symbolizing the couple being joined in union. Often these types of spoons would have a double bowl or would be flamboyantly carved. Occasionally, a joke spoon might be presented to the marital couple. With the two bowls arranged at impractical angles, this type of spoon would be nearly impossible to use for the sharing of a first meal; the couple would have to struggle mightily to make it work, much to the amusement of the assembled guests.

In common with the other spoon carving regions of Europe, the care and craftsmanship that went into a spoon told the young woman and her family a great deal about the young man's capabilities and character, so it was always important that a spoon be crafted to the very best of the carver's ability.

Simple Tester Spoons

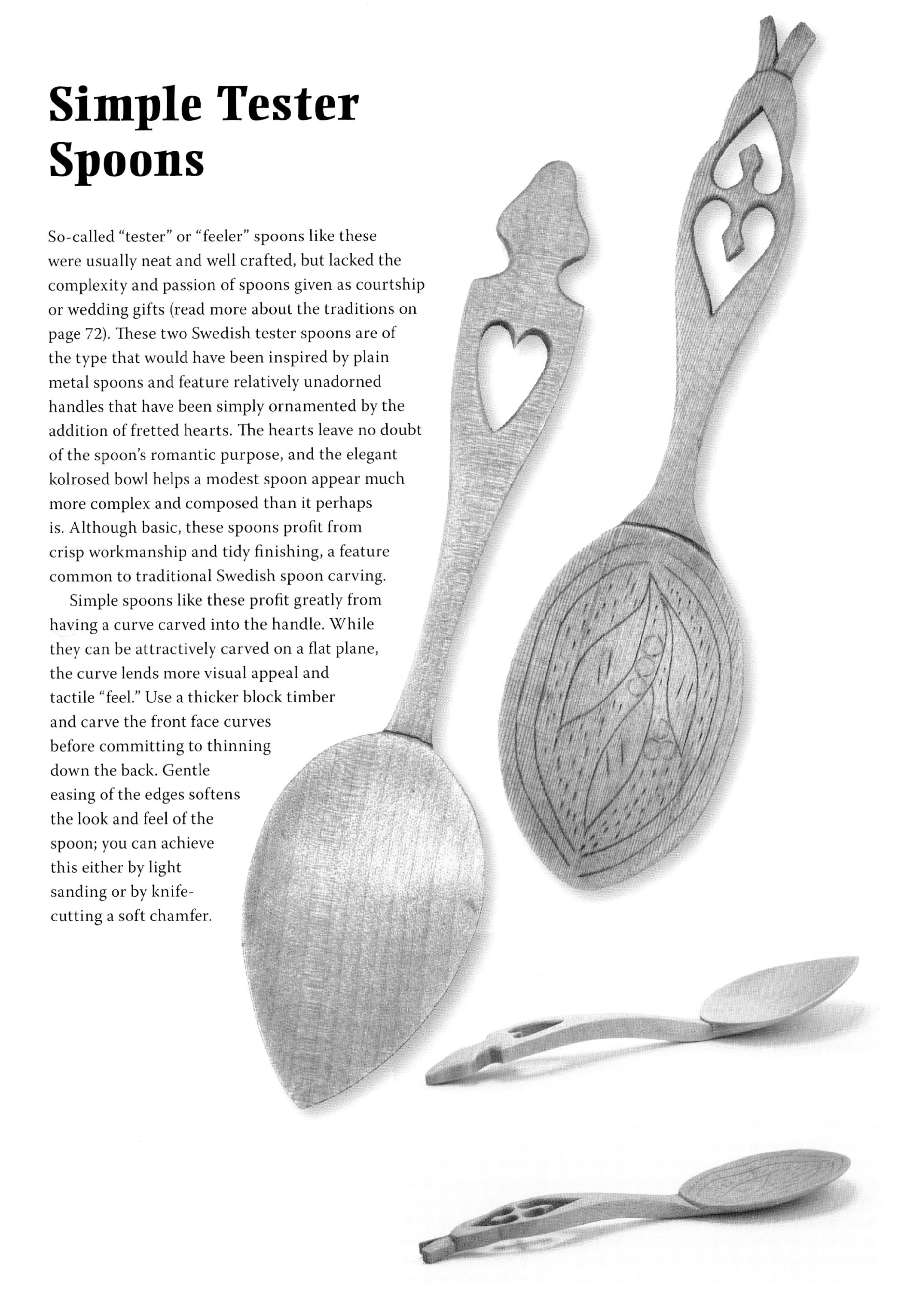

So-called "tester" or "feeler" spoons like these were usually neat and well crafted, but lacked the complexity and passion of spoons given as courtship or wedding gifts (read more about the traditions on page 72). These two Swedish tester spoons are of the type that would have been inspired by plain metal spoons and feature relatively unadorned handles that have been simply ornamented by the addition of fretted hearts. The hearts leave no doubt of the spoon's romantic purpose, and the elegant kolrosed bowl helps a modest spoon appear much more complex and composed than it perhaps is. Although basic, these spoons profit from crisp workmanship and tidy finishing, a feature common to traditional Swedish spoon carving.

Simple spoons like these profit greatly from having a curve carved into the handle. While they can be attractively carved on a flat plane, the curve lends more visual appeal and tactile "feel." Use a thicker block timber and carve the front face curves before committing to thinning down the back. Gentle easing of the edges softens the look and feel of the spoon; you can achieve this either by light sanding or by knife-cutting a soft chamfer.

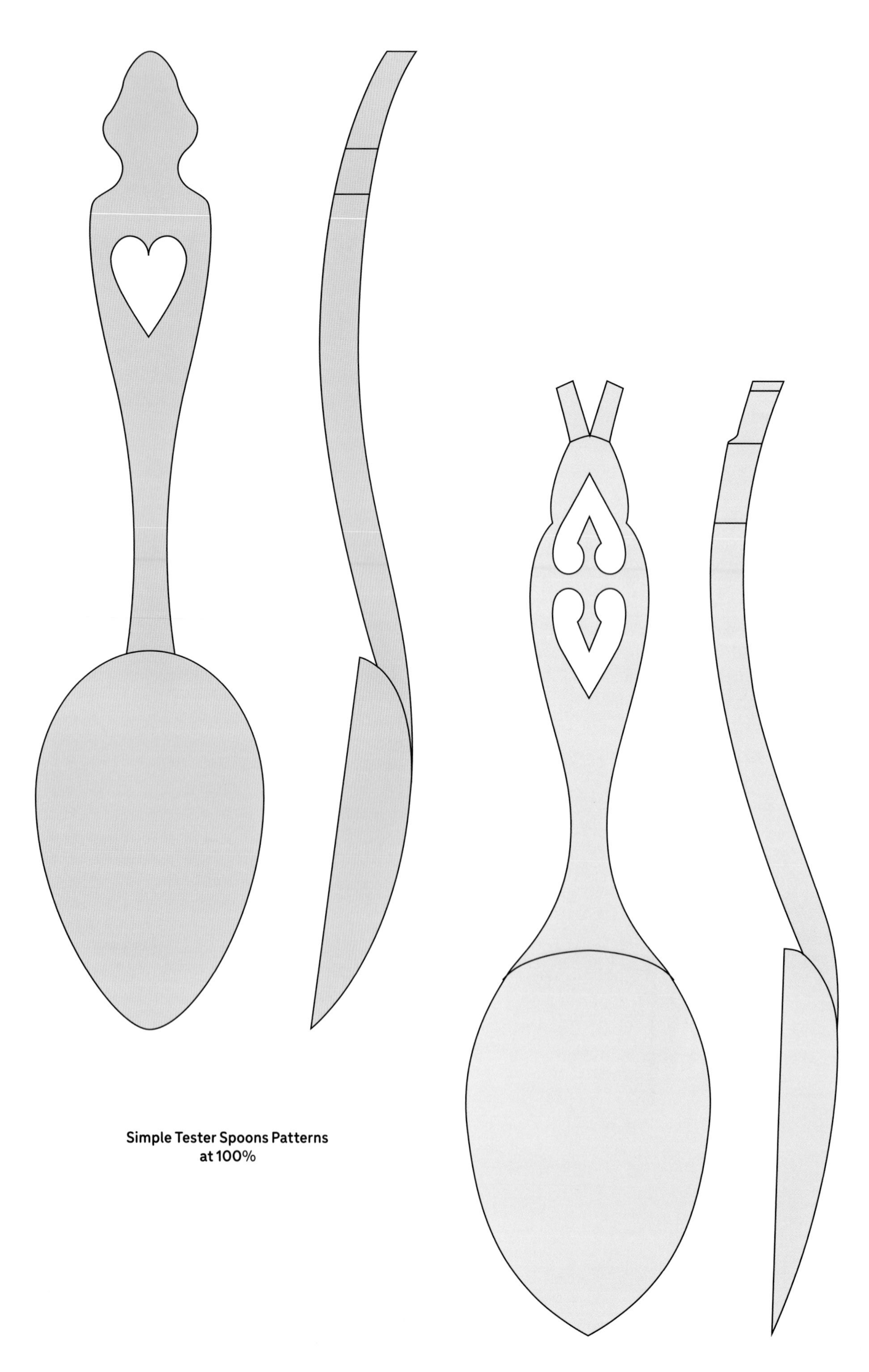

Simple Tester Spoons Patterns
at 100%

Long Hearts Spoon

This graceful design appears rudimentary at first glance, but it is actually remarkably refined. The perfectly placed protuberances on the long, sweeping handle add visual flair and are truly eye-catching. The finial detail at the crown is simple but wonderfully balanced and adds a sense of design sophistication to an otherwise modest spoon.

A spoon this elegant and developed is typical of the type of work of a professional or of a serious amateur with a very keen eye. A spoon like this would likely have been a much more significant gift than either of the spoons in the previous pair shown on page 73.

The two versions of this design amply illustrate the profound difference that wood color and figure can make toward a spoon's outcome. In this case, the dissimilarity between the dark straight-grained piece and the paler, flat-sawn one is so great that, at first glance, the spoons almost don't appear to be the same design. Even something as simple as gently rounding the edges (on the light spoon) versus keeping them square and sharp (on the dark spoon) has a significant effect on the spoon's final appearance.

This design works particularly well with a deeply curved handle and a tilted bowl. Many Swedish spoons feature an exaggerated angle where the bowl joins the stem that was achieved by utilizing wood taken from the area of a tree where a branch joins the main trunk.

Long Hearts Spoon Pattern
at 100%

Triple Crown Spoon

Swedish spoons are generally more conservative and less eclectic than their Welsh counterparts, but they frequently feature more variation in the shapes and sizes of their bowls. While Welsh lovespoons tend to almost exclusively feature the more egg-shaped, post-medieval bowl that we recognize as our modern spoon shape, Swedish spoons frequently have large and voluptuous round and oval shapes and occasionally even the reverse egg shape (with the point toward the handle) that was more common to medieval spoon design.

This sweet little courting spoon features a short, deeply tapered handle and an eye-catching three-leaf crown that has been balanced against a generous, broad oval bowl with a subtle point toward its stem end. The crown's leaves can be carved several ways. They can be stylized with a raised or lowered center (as shown), be cut flat or on an angle, or be shaped and detailed to mimic a realistic, natural leaf.

The bowl has been further ornamented with a delicate kolrosed pattern of etched lines combined with gouge and knife stab marks. When stabbing a design with a gouge, a single cut will leave a graceful curved line that can be repeated to form elegant patterns, or the gouge can be lightly spun to create a circular shape.

Triple Crown Spoon Pattern
at 100%

Pocket Tester Spoons

This set of spoons includes variations on a pair of simple tester spoon designs. The spoons would likely have been carried in a pocket during the time they were being crafted. They are relatively modest in both design and difficulty and represent the type of spoon that might have been made in multiples and given to several young women.

Each spoon has a dramatically curved handle, which helps to enhance the design and increase the visual sophistication of the finished spoon. The bowls mostly follow a more modern shaping, with the bowl's point at the end of the bowl furthest from the handle.

The double heart handles are only slightly different from each other in that one has a small diamond between the hearts and the other doesn't. The single heart handle differs more dramatically with its pair of raised "frames" ringing the handle.

Each spoon features a lovely organic fan detail at the crown that is simply formed by cutting an angled slope of approximately 40° onto each arm of the fan. Kolrosed bowls give the spoons some extra refinement.

Leave the junction between the stem and the bowl a bit thicker to add some strength to the weak area, especially if the stem is narrow at this point.

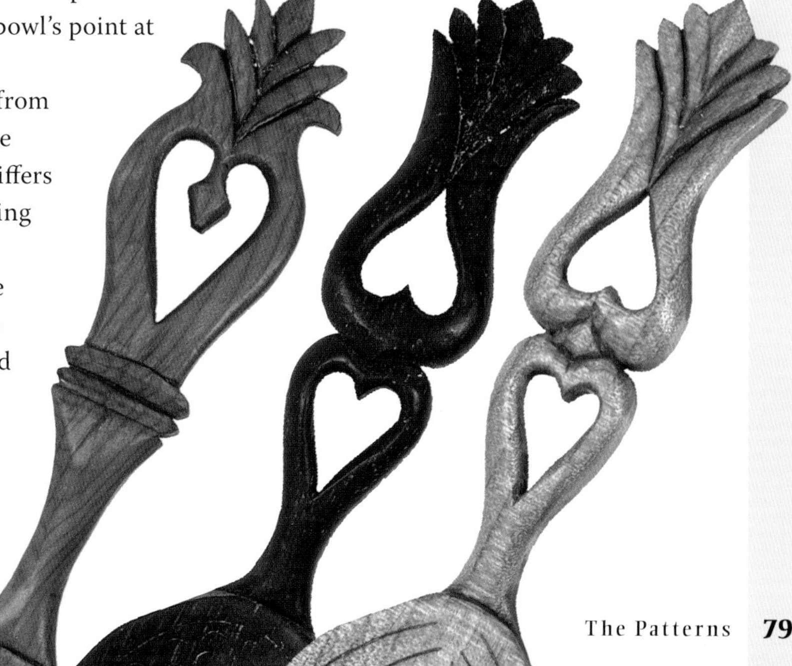

Pocket Tester Spoons Pattern at 100%

Pocket Tester Spoons Pattern at 100%

Four-Heart Courting Spoons

These three courting spoons are all based around a lovely four-heart motif that is very popular in both Swedish and Norwegian romantic woodcarving and that shows up in a wide variety of designs.

The first spoon (top) makes use of a very simple etched line to form a nice border that sweeps around the handle and gives an otherwise plain design a bit of finish. The top and bottom hearts are slightly larger than the side hearts, which allows the oval shape of the handle to be more evenly filled.

The second spoon (middle) uses more evenly sized hearts to fit a narrower handle shape. The spoon is bordered with a simple but elegant triangle chip pattern that is doubled through the center of the handle to form a slightly more complex design.

The third spoon (bottom) has the most regimented grouping of the four hearts, identical and strictly spaced. It also has a simple chip-carved triangle detail around the hearts, but a much more complex herringbone pattern along the stem. The small, generously curved handle is capped with a unique little tree-shaped crown.

Because all of the handles are quite small, take great care to cut the chip patterns consistently and carefully.

Four-Heart Courting Spoons Pattern
at 100%

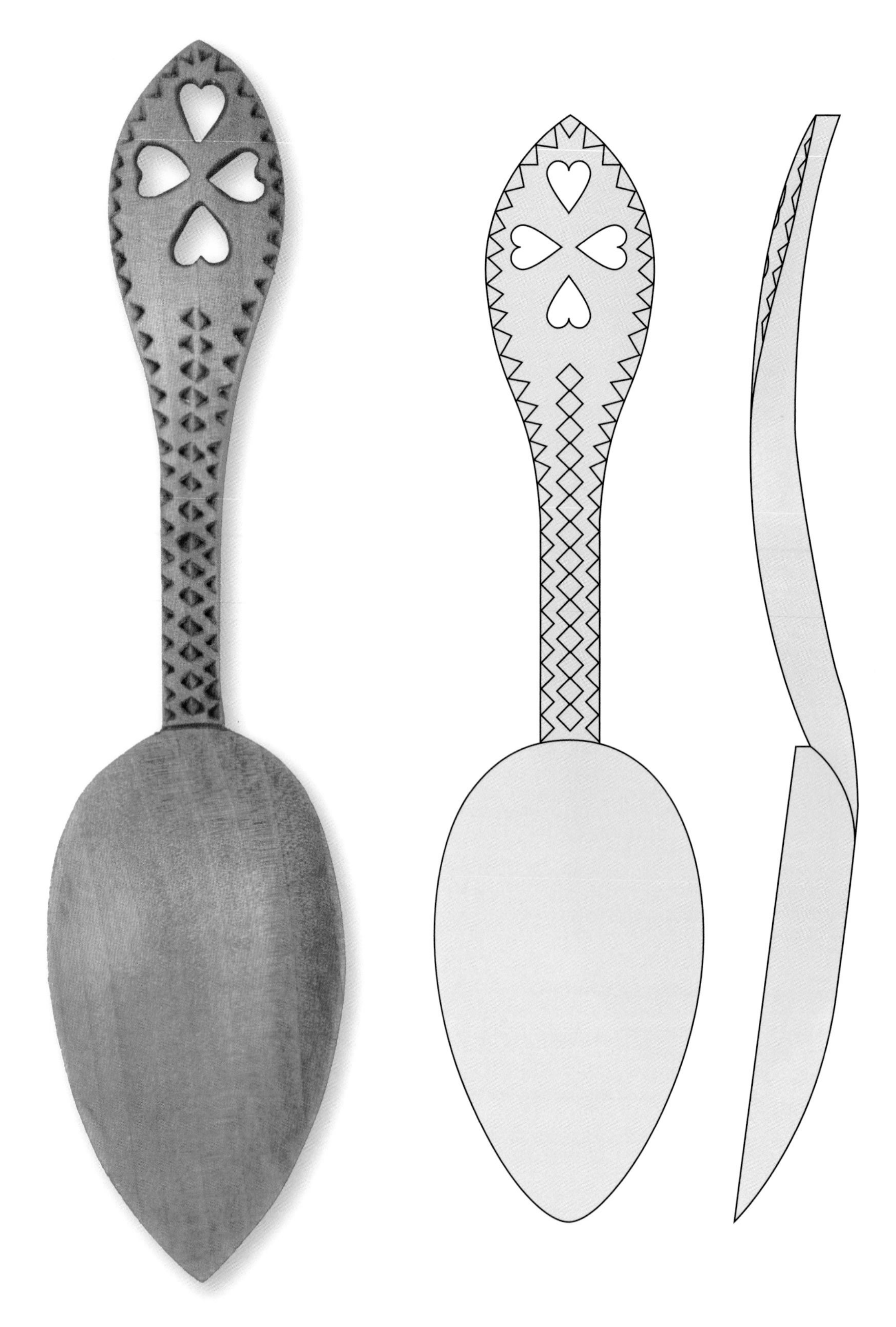

Four-Heart Courting Spoons Pattern
at 100%

Four-Heart Courting Spoons Pattern at 100%

Heart and Fan Spoon

Traditionally, a spoon like this would have been roughed out with an axe and then the majority of the carving undertaken with a sloyd knife (from the Swedish word *slöjd*, meaning craft or handicraft). These substantial knives are the backbone of Swedish woodcarving and can be used for everything from rough-shaping to fine detailing.

This uncomplicated tester-type spoon features freehand hearts and a lovely triangle chip-carved border. It has a fairly broad and thick stem that allows it to withstand heavy handling. The handle has been thinned from its thickest point at the bowl through to the crown of the handle. This thinning creates a much lighter feel than would be the case if the handle were left a consistent thickness throughout.

Take care when curving and doming to ensure the handle's symmetry and that the curving is fair without dips or rises.

Heart and Fan Spoon Pattern at 100%

Pinwheel Hearts Spoon

This substantial spoon makes use of both fretted detail and some beautiful chip-carved bordering and decoration to make a lovely courting spoon. The large, almost circular bowl has been left unadorned but would most certainly have been kolrosed before presentation to a young lady.

This particular spoon features a wonderfully unique border detail that can be marked out with the tip of a gouge or by freehand cutting with the tip of a straight knife. The lovely softness of the curves makes it an exceptionally attractive finish, and you can easily achieve it through basic chip-carving techniques.

The handle is very softly domed and runs fairly straight until just below the fretted hearts, where it curves deeply toward the bowl. Take care when shaping this detail not to take more off one side of the face surface of the handle and stem than the other—this would leave the spoon with a visible twist.

Swedish bowls are invariably professionally finished with evenly thin edges and fair curves inside and out. The bowl can be forgotten in the excitement of crafting a beautiful handle, but it is an essential and very important part of a well-done spoon. Bowls that are slightly asymmetrical, bumpy, or too thick always look awkward and are detrimental to the final appearance of the spoon.

To further enhance this spoon and increase the carving challenge, consider adding a small chain link or two at the crown.

Pinwheel Hearts Spoon Pattern
at 100%

Heart Spoons

This pair of romantic spoons illustrates two very different ways to handle a similar handle shape. On one, a large, fretted heart creates a much lighter-feeling handle, while on the other, a series of repeating hearts makes a much more solid and substantial design. The fretted spoon has a curved but un-domed handle, whereas the solid handle has been both heavily curved and domed to make it a bit more visual and voluptuous.

The repetitive heart is a bit more complicated than it appears at first glance. Each of the sections is both angled and slightly curved toward the next larger section, something that you must carve very carefully to avoid uneven areas or chip-outs. The fan detail on the fretted spoon is handled in much the same way as the repetitive hearts, but with much less difficulty caused by variations in grain direction.

Carving horses were once frequently employed (especially if the spoon was being carved by a professional carver or woodworker) to clamp the spoon blank firmly in place, with drawknives then used to undertake much of this type of shaping and curving work. Today, you're more likely to use a band saw or scroll saw to do much of this type of shaping.

Heart Spoons Pattern at 100%

Heart Spoons Pattern
at 100%

Flowing Spoons

Swedish spoon carvers were quite deft with their simple repetition of plant forms or symbols such as hearts. Repetition can create a powerful design much greater than the sum of its parts.

The plant-style handle here skillfully uses a variety of widths to add dynamism to a design that could rapidly become monotonous if all the leaves were exactly the same size. While this pattern might appear simple, the astute placement of the thicker leaves at the widest point of the handle's taper and the thinning of the leaves as they reach the stem are indicative of carefully considered and practiced design. The same can be said for the heart spoon.

The safest way to carve spoons like this is to shape the front face of the handle from a squared block and then undertake all the detailed carving. That way, you can put downward pressure on the carving without fear of snapping the handle. Once you have completed the carving of the front, shape the back down to its final thickness. Liberally round the leaves and the hearts to help soften the overall appearance of the spoon and define each section.

While a thin stem looks best on the heart design, it does weaken the spoon considerably at the bowl. Leave a bit of extra thickness on the stem in order to lend a good deal of support to the fragile area.

Flowing Spoons Pattern
at 100%

Flowing Spoons Pattern
at 100%

Pinwheel Spoon

This modest design is indicative of the type of spoon a young man might carry with him to work on during quiet moments. It is a fairly simple but robust design that favors chip-carved patterning over fretted work. The result is a slightly stout and structurally solid piece that uses a well-rounded taper and a sharply pointed crown to lighten the visual appearance a bit. As with many Swedish spoons, there is a healthy curve and some light doming to the handle, some taper to the bowl, and a bit of extra thickness to support the stem.

You can easily undertake this design with only a straight knife for the handle detailing and the shaping of the back of the bowl and a hook knife for hollowing out the front face of the bowl. Use a sharp and pointy straight knife for rendering the chip-carved patterns, especially for getting the pinwheel pattern clean and neat.

If you're using wood with a figure and tone as vigorous as it is in this piece, leave the bowl unadorned, without the traditional kolrosing. Colorful and vibrant woods make kolrosing look lost and somewhat redundant.

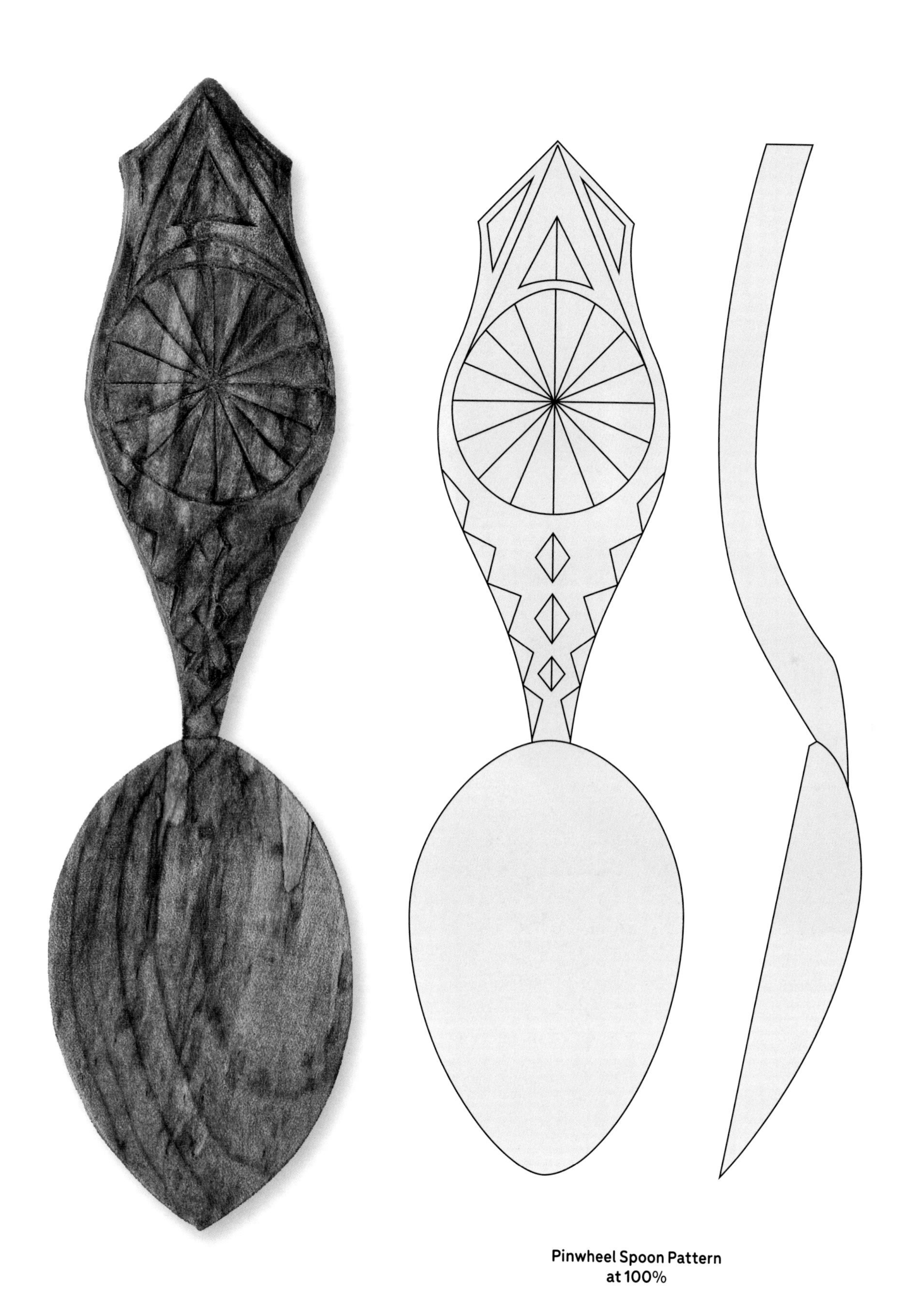

Pinwheel Spoon Pattern at 100%

Fretted Shield Spoon

This superb panel-style courting spoon is a fabulous example of the type of high skill and excellent design sense for which Swedish romantic spoon carvers were renowned. The fretwork makes a stocky handle appear wonderfully light and airy, with the unique inverted heart at the crown drawing the eye through the spoon and to the tip. A spoon of this quality would most likely have had some kolrosed patterning in the spoon bowl, but the impressive figure and birds-eye knot structure of this piece of yew wood lends the piece more than enough visual drama.

This spoon has been carved from a thick piece of timber with the top of the handle left flat and a striking curve to the bowl livening up the piece quite considerably. The handle has been left a tiny bit thicker than would be common on Welsh or Breton spoons, which protects the delicate fretted work and gives the panel increased strength. The back of the handle could be gently domed to create the illusion of a thin handle while maintaining structural support.

Lightly round the heart at the crown to create a more voluptuous feel and to contrast slightly with the sharply squared edges of the rest of the handle design. Also leave some thickness at the back of the bowl where the stem joins it, as the narrowness of the stem combined with the diamond cutout weakens the structure.

Fretted Shield Spoon Pattern at 100%

Knotwork Spoons

This lovely knotwork design likely has its roots in the long-ago merging of Celtic and Viking art. A popular motif in Scandinavian woodcarving, the knot shows up in both Swedish and Norwegian spoon designs. The two examples shown here illustrate how different the more rounded knot appears from the flatter and squarer version, as well as how the addition of simple flourishes, such as the crown fan or the chip-carved stem, can alter the feel of the design.

To maximize the effect of the knotwork, cut the overs and unders of the knot crisply and consistently, making sure the ribbons of the knotwork remain as even in width as possible. The knotwork will appear to greatest effect if both the front and back of the handle are shaped. However, you must take care to ensure the back face is correctly carved so the overs and unders are exactly opposite to the front.

The simpler of the two spoons has significant damage at the tip of the bowl. This is a typical breakage that appears on many antique romantic spoons and is generally the result of the spoon falling from its place on a wall and striking the floor.

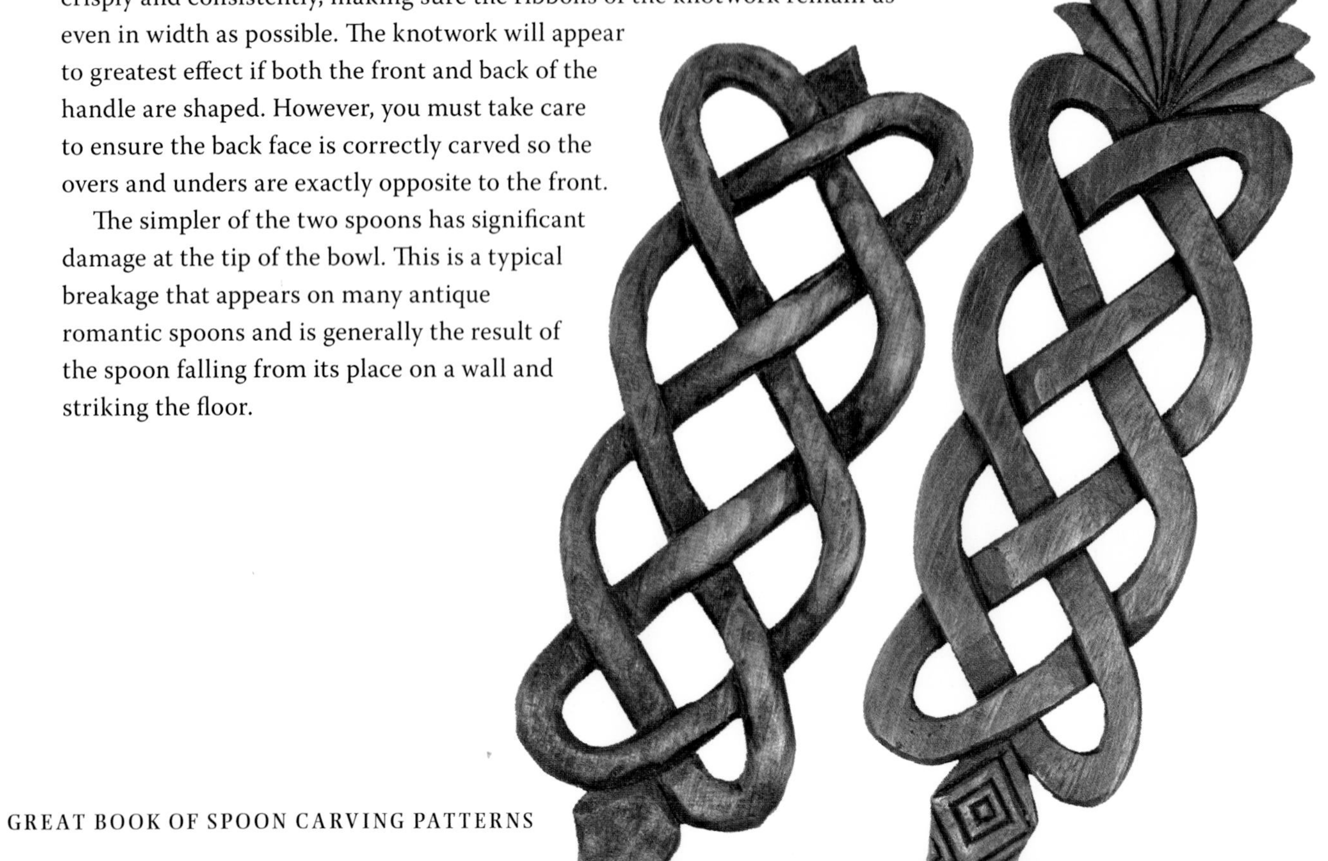

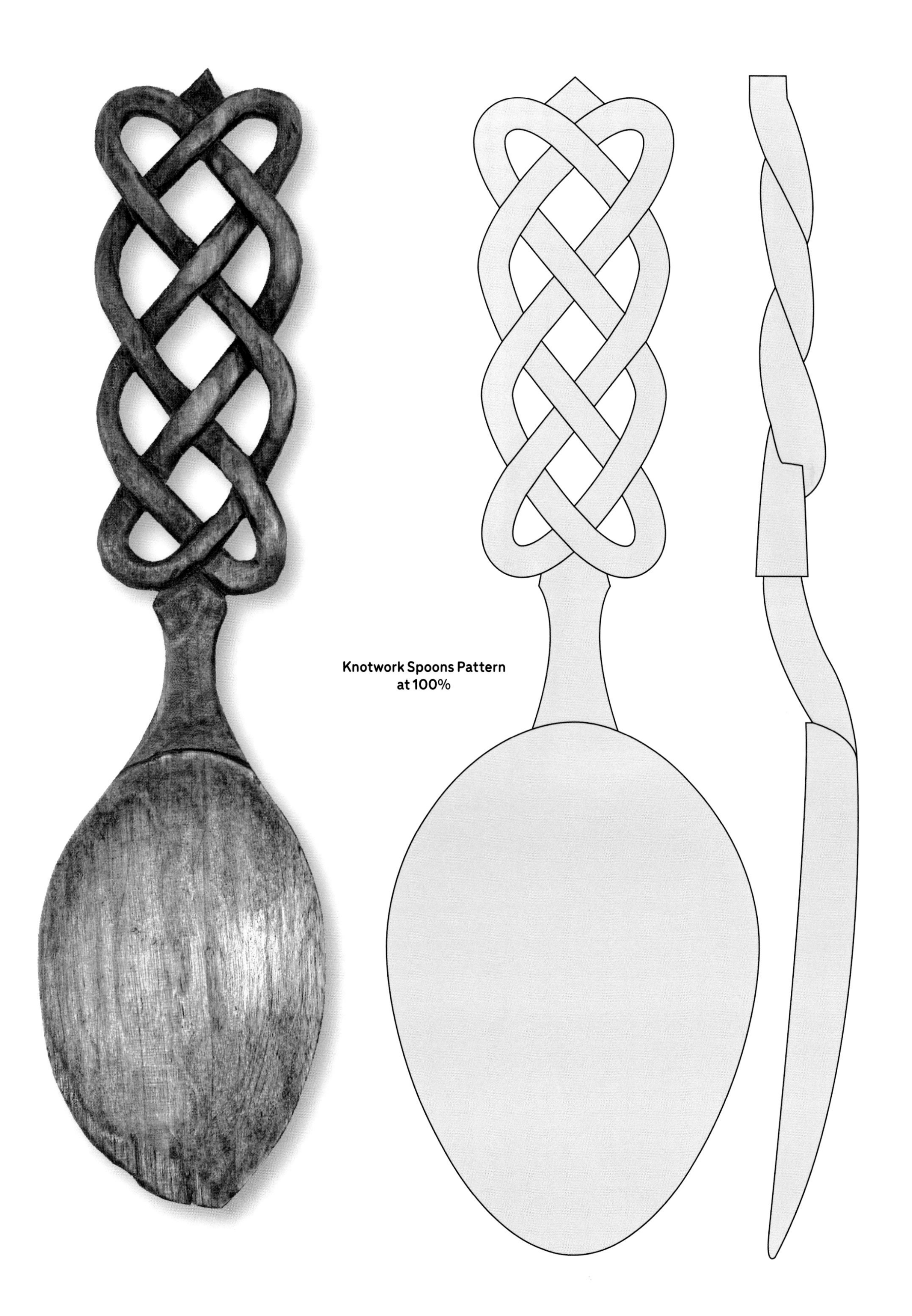
Knotwork Spoons Pattern
at 100%

Knotwork Spoons Pattern
at 100%

Simple Passion Spoon

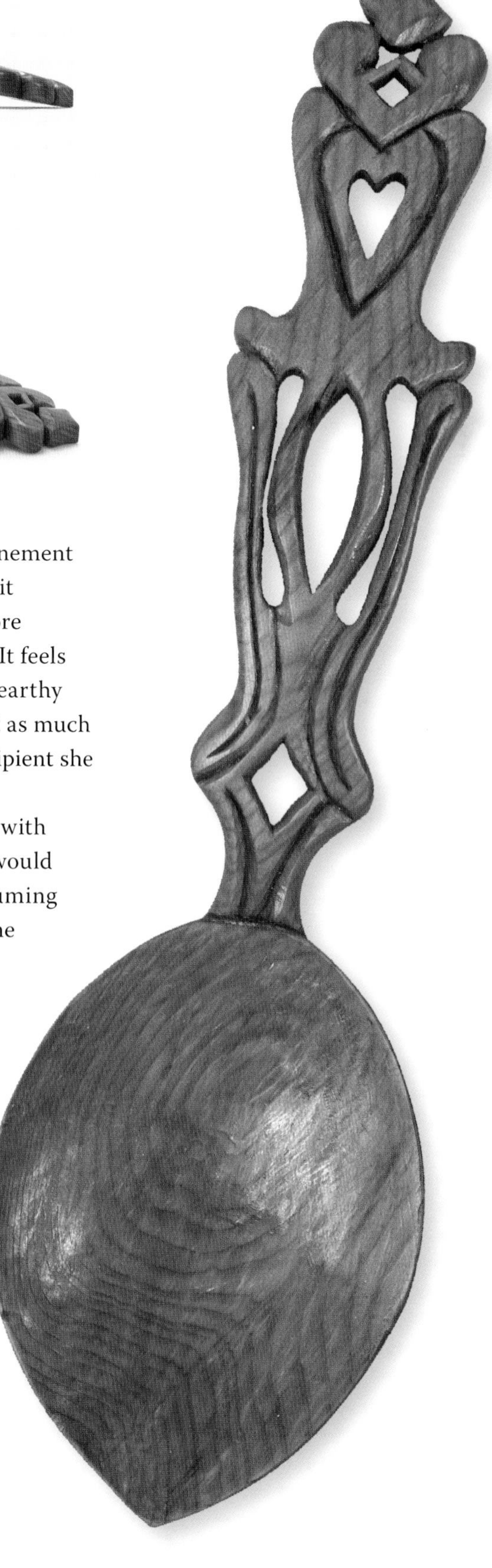

While this long, narrow-handled spoon lacks some of the refinement and heightened craft skill of many Swedish romantic spoons, it nevertheless has a charming visual passion about it that is more reminiscent of the eclectic appearance of a Welsh lovespoon. It feels remarkably spontaneous and is lively and engaging as well as earthy and ardent. This isn't a spoon that is trying to be a work of art as much as one that is wearing its heart on its sleeve and telling its recipient she is the object of love and infatuation.

Although fretwork of this nature can be easily undertaken with modern scroll saws or hand-held jeweler's saws, originally, it would have been done with the tip of a straight knife. It's time-consuming work, but with limited access to tools, it is simply how old-time Swedish carvers would have had to do it.

Slightly round the exterior edges of the handle and the edges around the fretwork to give the spoon a much softer look and feel than it would have if the edges were left square. Try not to get carried away cutting the "pinstriping" lines that flow along the handle—cutting too deep or wide in this area can make the stripes too distracting.

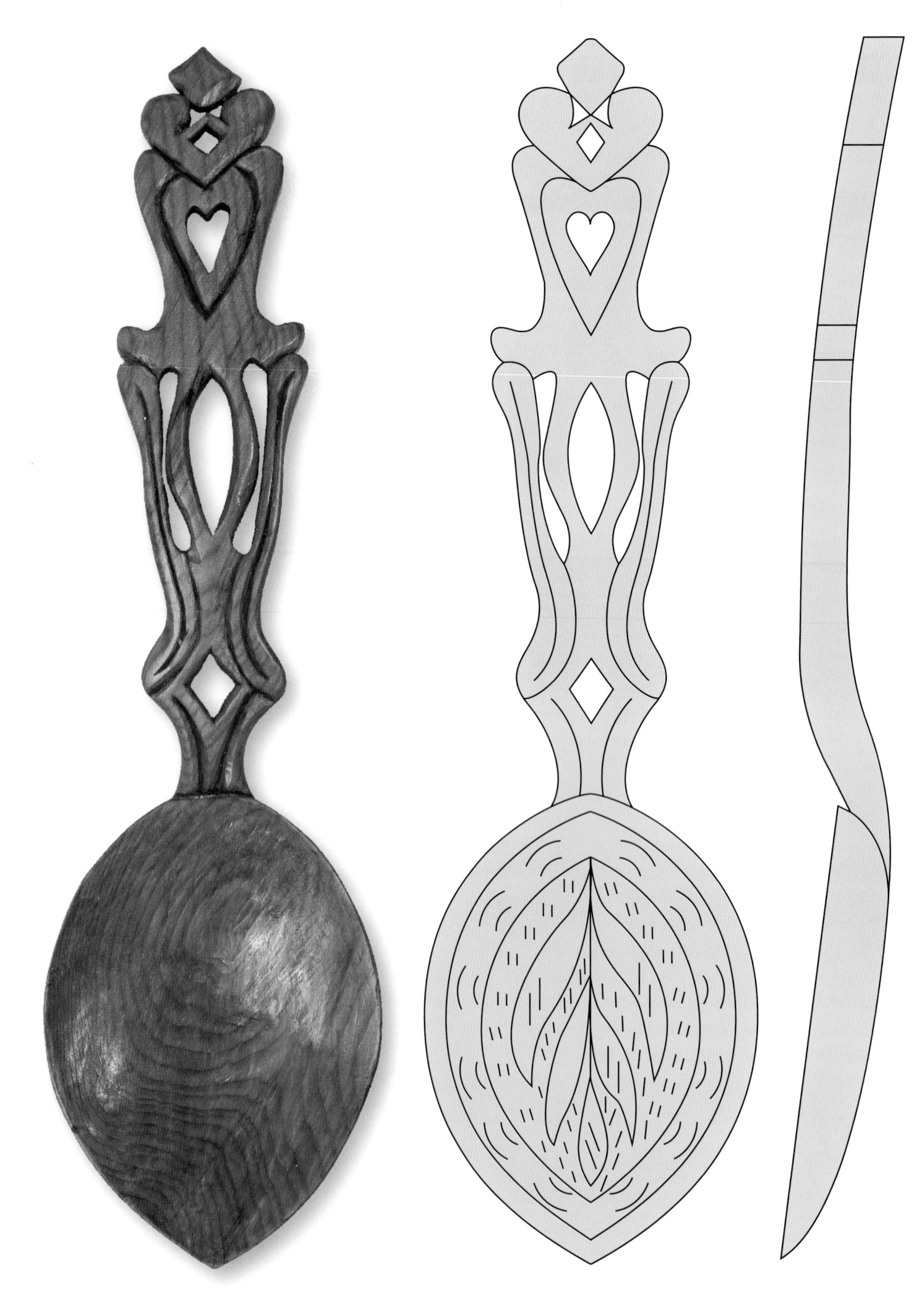

Simple Passion Spoon Pattern
at 100%

Rings of Love Spoon

A courting spoon such as this would have been a significant gift, expressing both the young man's passion and his abundant abilities. This spoon is more of a technical challenge than it might appear at first glance and represents a much more serious gift than some of the previous Swedish spoon designs in this book.

The rings and steep handle curve require working from a thick block of wood, so take care at the roughing-out stage not to remove too much stock and weaken the stem, while still clearing sufficient material to enable the fretting and link shaping.

When shaping the top links, start by making one thick link and then subdividing it into two thin rings at the very end of the carving. Making a single thick ring is easier carving, and its mass will protect it against accidental breakage, which is always a danger when the rings are as delicate as these. This spoon could also be carved without the rings and still be beautiful.

Complete the border detail before undertaking too much fretting or removal of stock from the back of the handle. Leave the back solid and square until the front has been fully shaped and detailed. This will enable the piece to be securely clamped to a workbench if required and will offer lots of structural support against excessive downward carving pressure.

Rings of Love Spoon Pattern
at 100%

Wedding Rings Spoon

The lovely reindeer horn wedding spoons carved by the Sami people of Northern Scandinavia are the likely source of inspiration for this beautiful courting/dowry–type spoon. Sami spoons feature a horn handle and bowl with tiny metal or horn rings that run along the side, a feat that has been mimicked with slightly larger wooden rings in this example.

This technically remarkable spoon is of the type intended to impress the young woman's family as much as the woman herself. It would have been solid proof that the young man was both capable and tenacious and that his passion for the young woman was beyond question.

The timber required to craft this design needs to be thick enough to form circular rings and enable you to execute a good amount of curved and domed shaping along the handle and stem.

Carving the sideways rings presents a number of challenges. The grain orientation through the ring can become extremely weak if the loop is carved at a strict 90-degree angle to the handle, so align the link as much as possible with the handle's grain direction. Even when aligned as much as possible with the handle's grain, the links will still be somewhat weak structurally, so be gentle while carving.

As with most Swedish romantic spoons of high quality, the bowl would have been lavishly ornamented with kolrosing. In this particular case, though, the strong grain pattern in this spoon's bowl is vivid enough in its own right and so has been left unadorned.

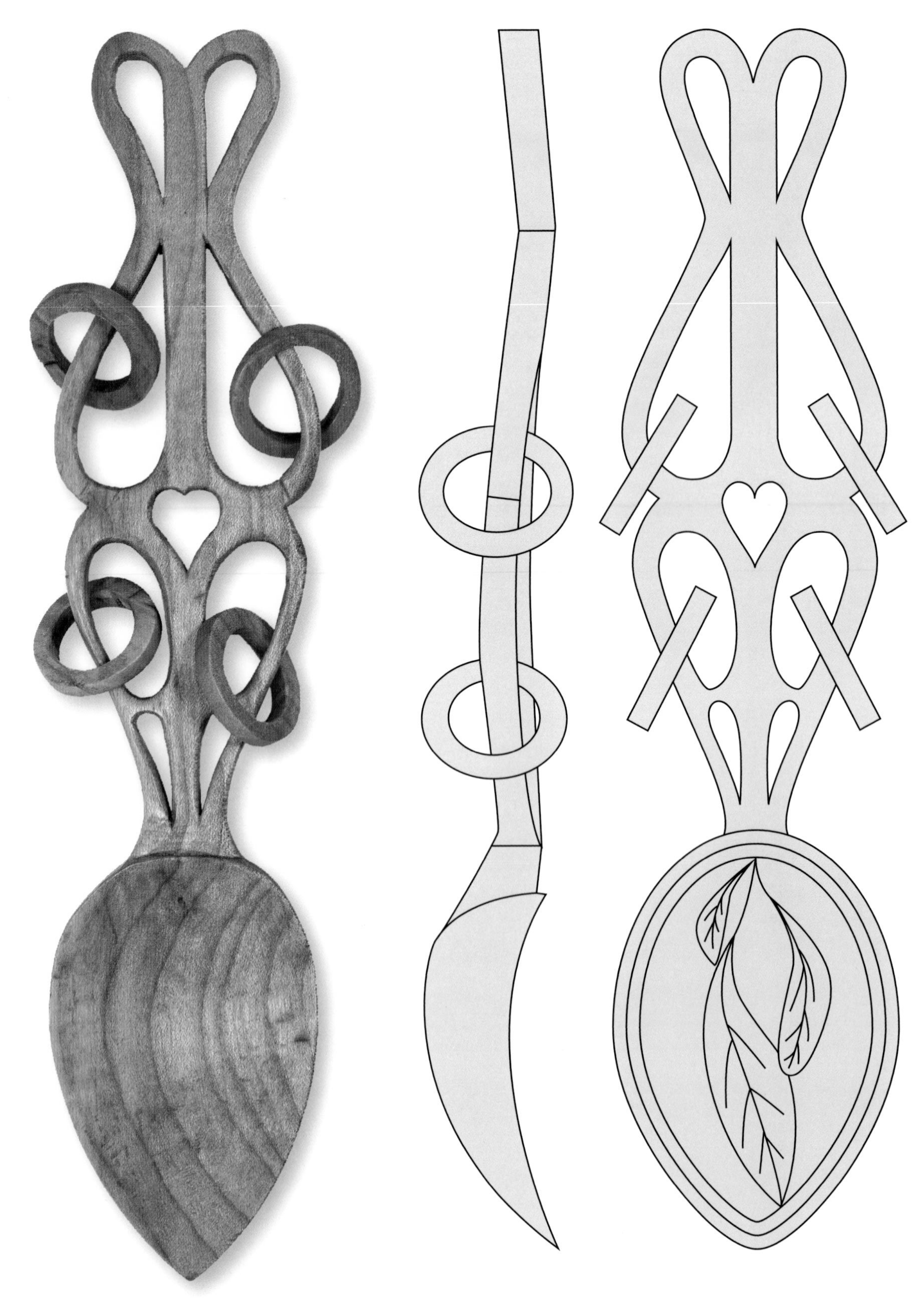

Wedding Rings Spoon Pattern at 100%

Wales

The best known of all the European romantic spoon types, Welsh lovespoons are renowned for their dramatic shapes and eclectic range of design styles. A tradition in Wales since at least the mid-1600s, lovespoons were carved to initiate a courtship and, judging by the level of effort demonstrated in most of the museum pieces, were probably gifted when a positive response was most likely.

Although there is no evidence that they were considered a betrothal gift, Welsh lovespoons were a much more serious offering than some of the more simply carved spoons in other regions of Europe that were given more to "test the waters" than in expectation of a serious reaction.

While most Welsh lovespoons were carved by lovestruck amateurs, there is ample evidence that professional carvers became involved in the tradition as well. Likely, those young men who were all thumbs would organize an exchange of skills, products, or money to ensure they had a competitive spoon to give their sweethearts.

Welsh lovespoon carving nearly died out at the start of the 1900s, along with most other types of wooden love token carving. Fortunately, it persisted in the isolated rural areas of the country before being embraced by the souvenir industry as an icon of Wales. Today, even though they have helped to revitalize the tradition, the mass-produced spoons churned out by commercial ventures are about as far from the original Welsh lovespoon's meaning and appearance as it is possible to get. Unfortunately, the overwhelming presence and mundane designs of these modern commercial spoons have led the average person to a mistaken belief that they truly represent the lovespoon tradition.

The Welsh designs included here follow traditional styles as closely as possible and accurately represent the various types of lovespoons crafted during the golden age of Welsh carving. The patterns include simple designs from the beginning of the lovespoon era; thin-handled designs that reflect when carvers began incorporating tricks such as chain links and ball-in-cage; broad, panel-style patterns that allowed ardent carvers the space to indulge in ever more elaborate flights of fancy; and intricately fretted designs that became possible in the later years of the 1800s with the advent of affordable jeweler's saws and scroll saws.

Cwtch Bach (Little Cuddle) Spoon

Welsh lovespoon lore suggests that the lovespoon evolved from the common Welsh eating spoon (known as a *cawl* spoon for the famous Welsh stew). While it seems a plausible hypothesis, virtually none of the hundreds of antique spoons housed in museums or private collections back this theory up. From the earliest dated spoon in the collection of the Welsh National History Museum at St Fagans (1667) through to spoons of Victorian or Edwardian vintage, almost none have the cawl spoon's distinctive broad bowl. Instead, their bowls mimic more closely the egg-shaped spoon bowl common to the newly in-vogue metal spoon, suggesting that the romantically carved lovespoon began as more an attempt to emulate fashionable metal spoons than to expand on the eating spoon.

This design, based on an early, simple spoon, has the more egg-shaped bowl and two of the most commonly seen traditional symbols: the heart for love and the diamond for prosperity. A simple but very effective chip-carved diamond pattern lends the stem of the spoon a little bit of pizzazz.

This design can easily be carved with the simplest of tools, but if shaping with an axe, serious caution is required in the area of the long, thin stem. To ensure structural strength and minimize the danger of breakage, leave this area largely unworked until most of the other carving is complete. Some delicate chip-carved patterning along the stem will lend the spoon some extra sophistication, but don't cut the pattern too deeply in this already weakened area. In the old days, the fretted patterns would be cleared out by cutting through with a straight knife. Use a drill to rough out material and save a great deal of knife cutting; use a scroll or jeweler's saw to save even more.

Cwtch Bach (Little Cuddle)
Spoon Pattern
at 100%

Y Llwyau Metel (The Metal Spoons)

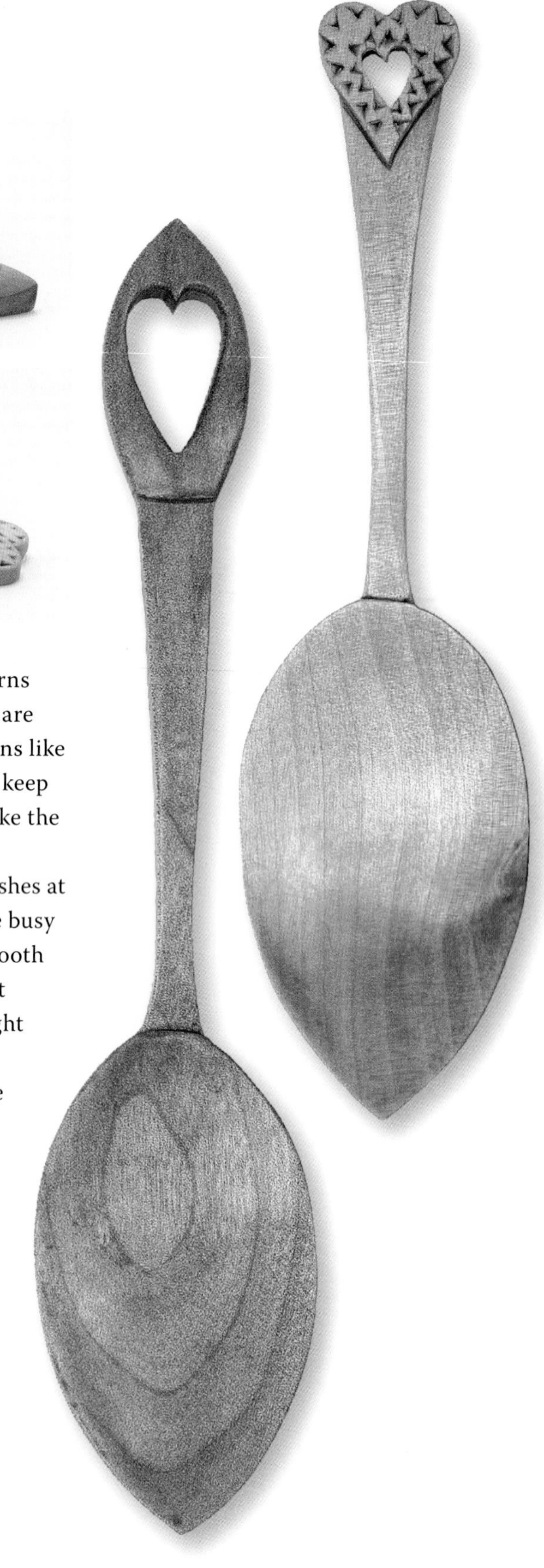

Here are two more designs heavily influenced by metal spoon patterns and handle styles. The thin, gently tapering handles are elegant but are more fragile than those found on traditional eating spoons, so spoons like these were likely made more for show than for use. That said, if you keep the handle a bit thicker where it passes into the bowl, you could make the spoon much more robust and usable.

Although these designs are both extremely basic, the little flourishes at the crown elevate their appearance considerably. On one spoon, the busy chip-carved pattern of the heart contrasts wonderfully with the smooth elegance of the simple handle. On the other, the entire spoon is kept smooth and in keeping with the flow of the handle, but with the slight ballooning of its crown becomes eye-catching and unique.

These spoons can be carved from thin, flat stock, but you can use a thicker timber and arch the handle a bit to give the spoon a much more vibrant appearance in line with the gentle curve of a metal spoon. Both of these spoons can be easily carved using only a straight knife for the handle and a bent knife for the bowl.

Because the crowns of both spoons are so small, there is not a great deal of room for decoration. On the chip-carved version, careful layout and even cutting is essential. Keep the triangular chip cuts to about 1⁄16 inch (1.5mm) or less in each direction.

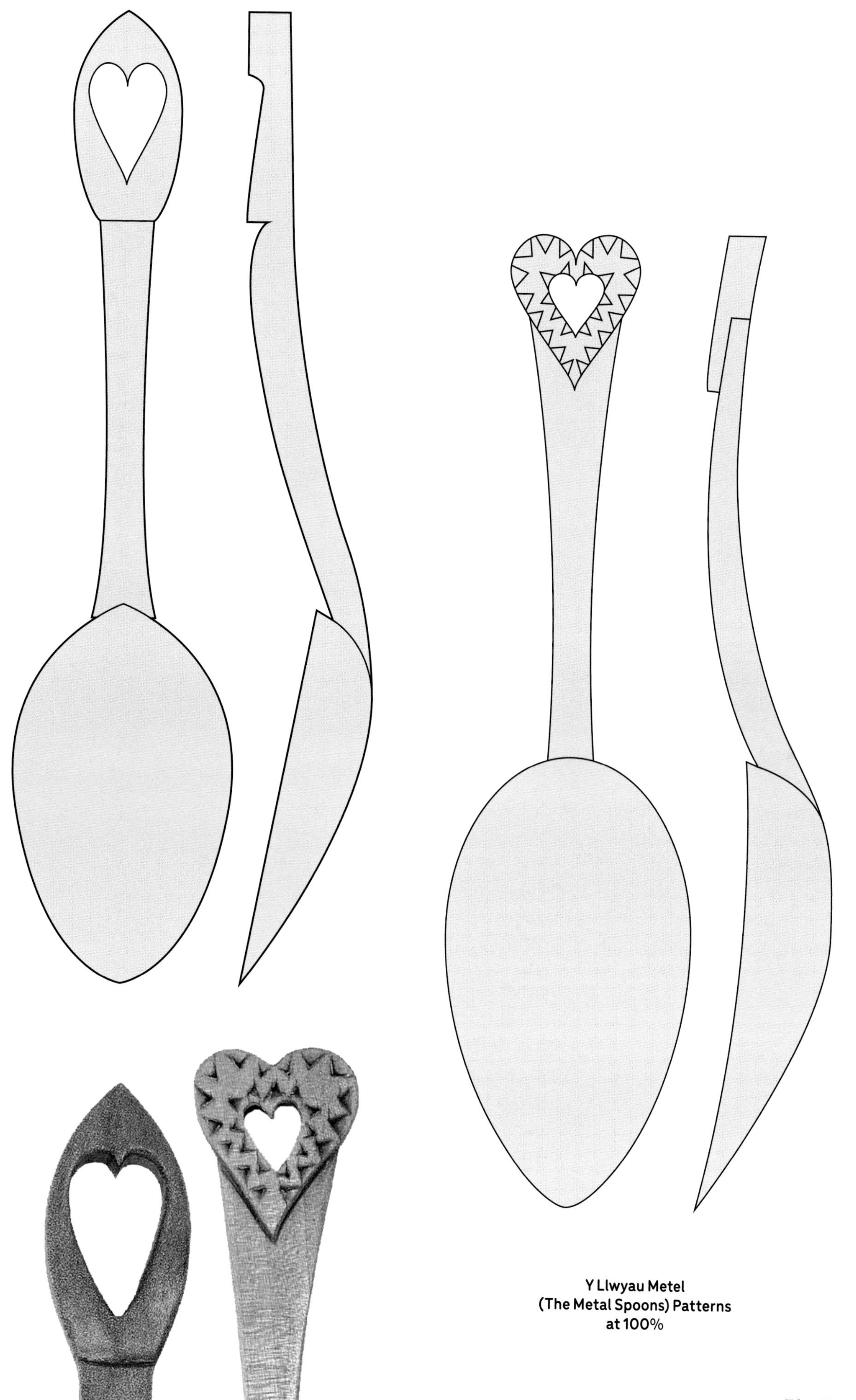

Y Llwyau Metel
(The Metal Spoons) Patterns
at 100%

Roese Spoon

The influence of the metal spoon is clearly felt in the design of this modest and romantic little spoon. Its slender, elegant handle, gracefully curved crown detail, and sweeping stem are typical of the metal spoons of the 1600s and 1700s. The egg-shaped bowl also has more in common with the metal spoon than with the traditional Welsh cawl (soup) spoon.

Back in the early days of lovespoon carving, the carver would have had a straight knife, an axe, and possibly a homemade curved knife (in Welsh called a *twca cam,* which roughly translates to "bent dagger") that would have been fashioned from a bucket handle or broken plowshare. The elegant curves of the crown would have been hand-shaped using the bent knife, while the straight knife would have been used to shape the stem.

You will need a fairly thick piece of timber—minimum ¾ inch (1.9cm)—in order to accommodate the curved stem and the sweeping crown detail. The area at the top of the fretted heart can easily break if the spoon is roughly handled during carving, so work slowly and cautiously in this area and support the spoon as much as possible to guard against torquing and stressing the area.

Due to its lack of adornment, this design shows equally well carved into an attractively figured piece of wood or into one that is quite plain and homogenous.

Roese Spoon Pattern
at 100%

Chip-Carved Heart Spoons

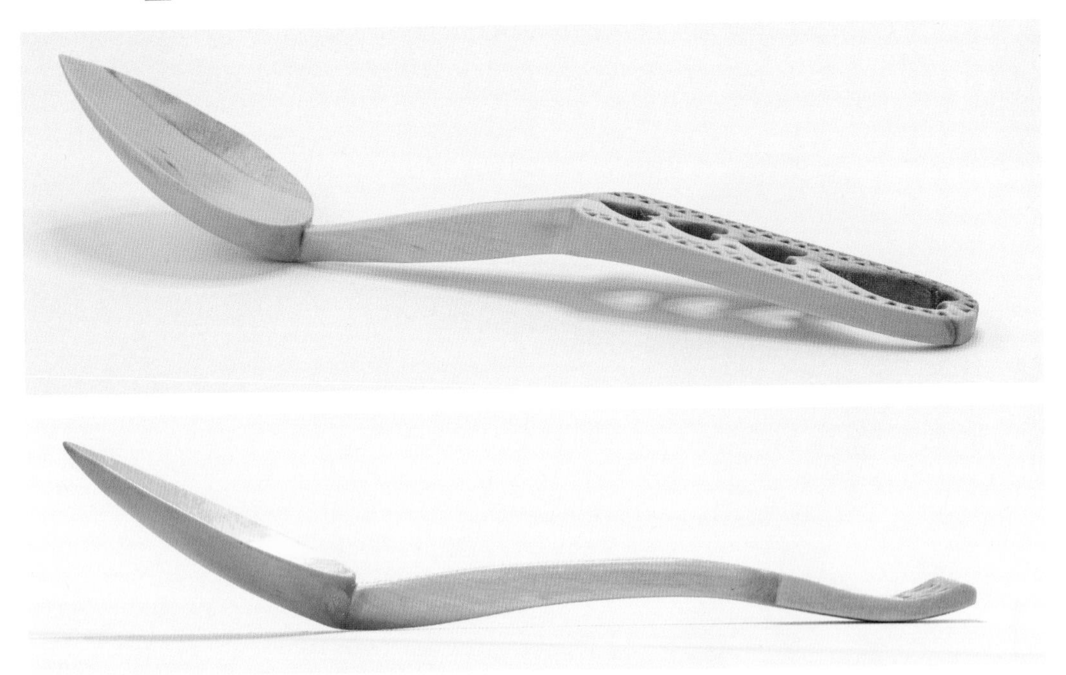

This pair of spoons display metal spoon design features, with their long, slender, and slightly tapering handles that culminate in ornately decorated crowns. They also both feature prominent hearts; in the early days of Welsh lovespoon carving, the heart was the foremost symbol, both in the frequency with which it appears and the power of its symbolic statement.

In the multi-heart spoon, the recurrence of the heart motif combined with the careful repetition of the chip-carved border lends the design a heightened level of thoughtfulness and elegance. The spoon gains further visual appeal from the use of light and dark grain through the center of the handle. Contrasting grain, figure, or color can add a great deal of additional vibrancy to any finished spoon. This spoon also features a sharp angle change from the flat of the handle to the taper of the stem. This may be a nod to metal spoon design, or it may have just been a nice way to add some excitement to the curve of the stem.

On the single-heart spoon, the crown section is delicately carved with a chip border and an incised heart. It also has a lovely sweep that hints at metal spoon origins. Handle the curve at the crown with a bent knife or carving gouges to avoid the "digging in" that a straight blade would invariably make in this area.

For either spoon, if you are chip carving into a softer wood, make sure your blades are razor-sharp to avoid tearing cross-grain sections.

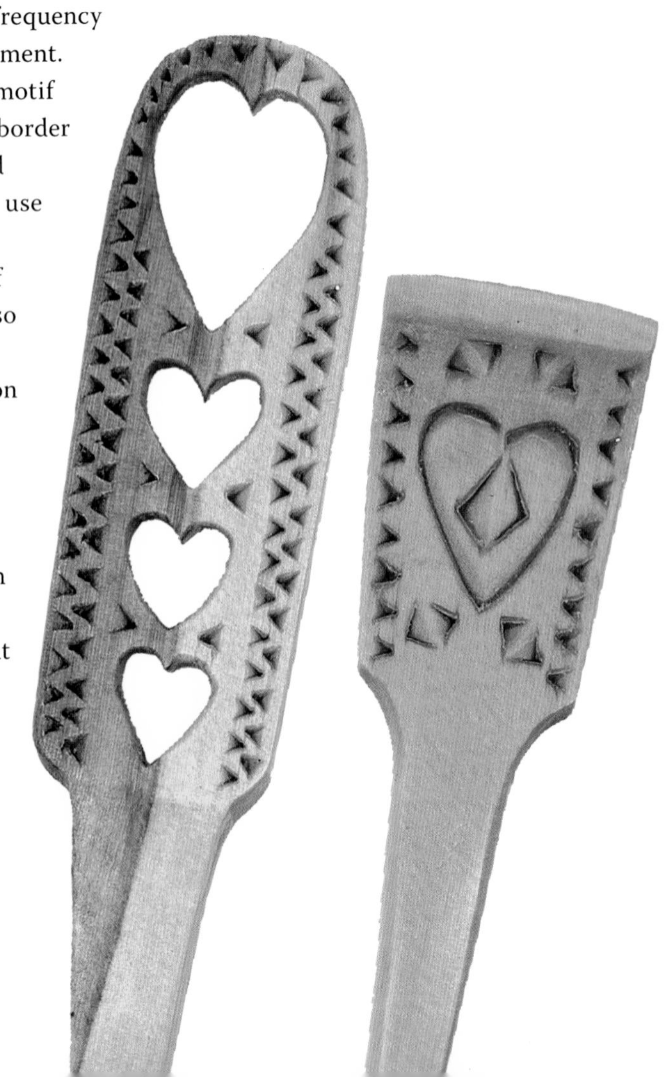

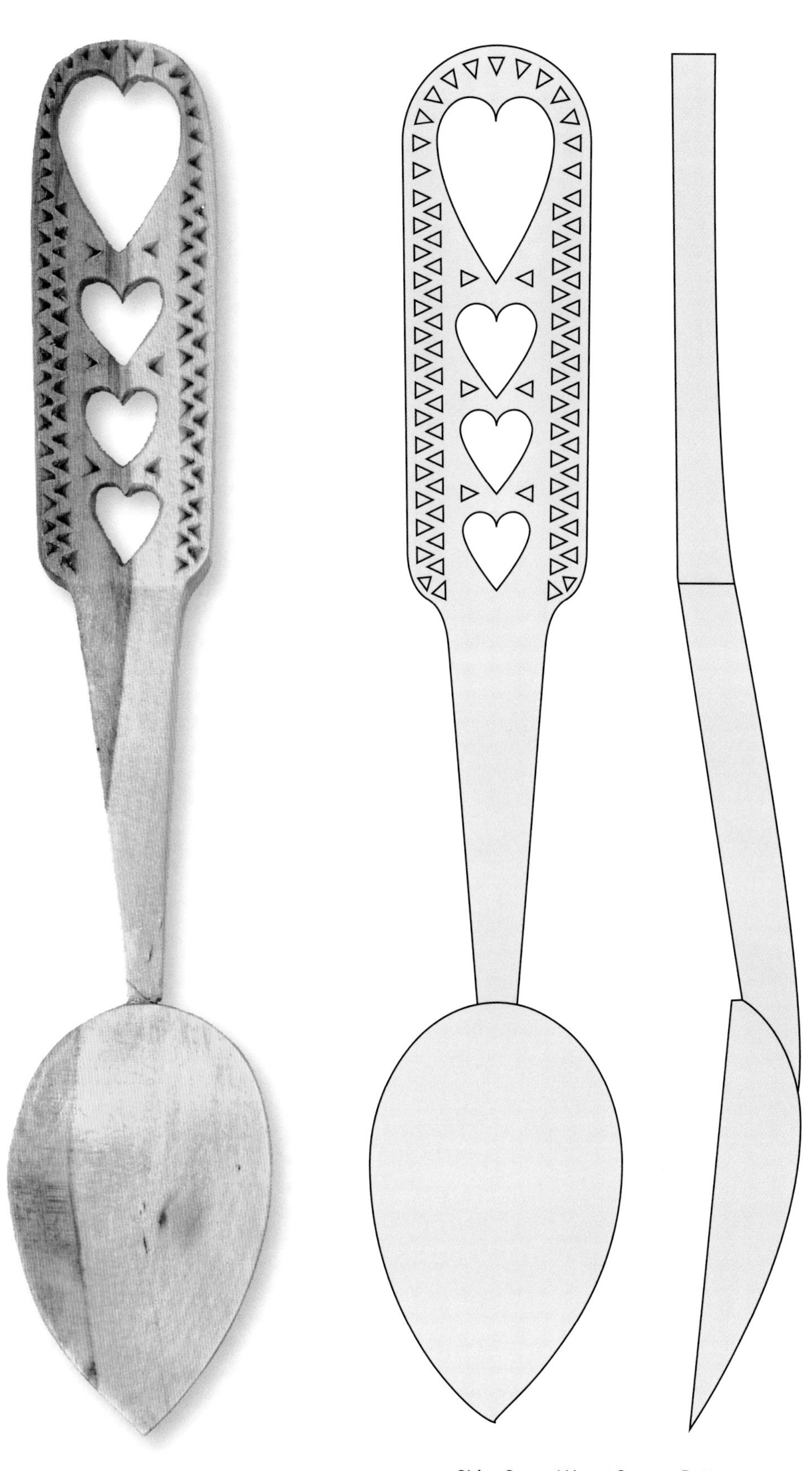

Chip-Carved Heart Spoons Pattern at 100%

Chip-Carved Heart Spoons Pattern
at 100%

Rustic Spoon

This spoon, while extremely simple in design, is interesting because it shows some influence from metal spoon design, but also illustrates the early development of the wider-handle lovespoon style that has become popular to this day.

Two fretted hearts and two unusual fretted areas of unknown meaning (fretted areas like this often just followed the flow of the design and had no symbolic message) form a lovely, slightly wider handle with a graceful crown and curving taper. In the old days, the fretted sections would have been cut away with the tip of a straight knife and would likely have been a bit less symmetrical and neat than the ones on this example. Despite being rustic and a bit untidy, the hand-cut fretted patterns often had a liveliness and spontaneity that can be missing if the carving is too neat and ordered. Even the simplest of Welsh spoons inevitably feature a really well-carved and thoughtfully finished bowl. Though you may be tempted to overlook the bowl a bit, remember that it is something of a point of pride to carve them well.

The spoon has a bucolic feel and seems more inspired by passion than by a conscious desire to mimic metal designs or be overly artistic. This particular spoon was carved from a small, thin piece of yew wood and would have likely benefitted from a bit more curve through the handle. Nevertheless, it's a wonderful, evocative little spoon that certainly utilizes simplicity to a great end.

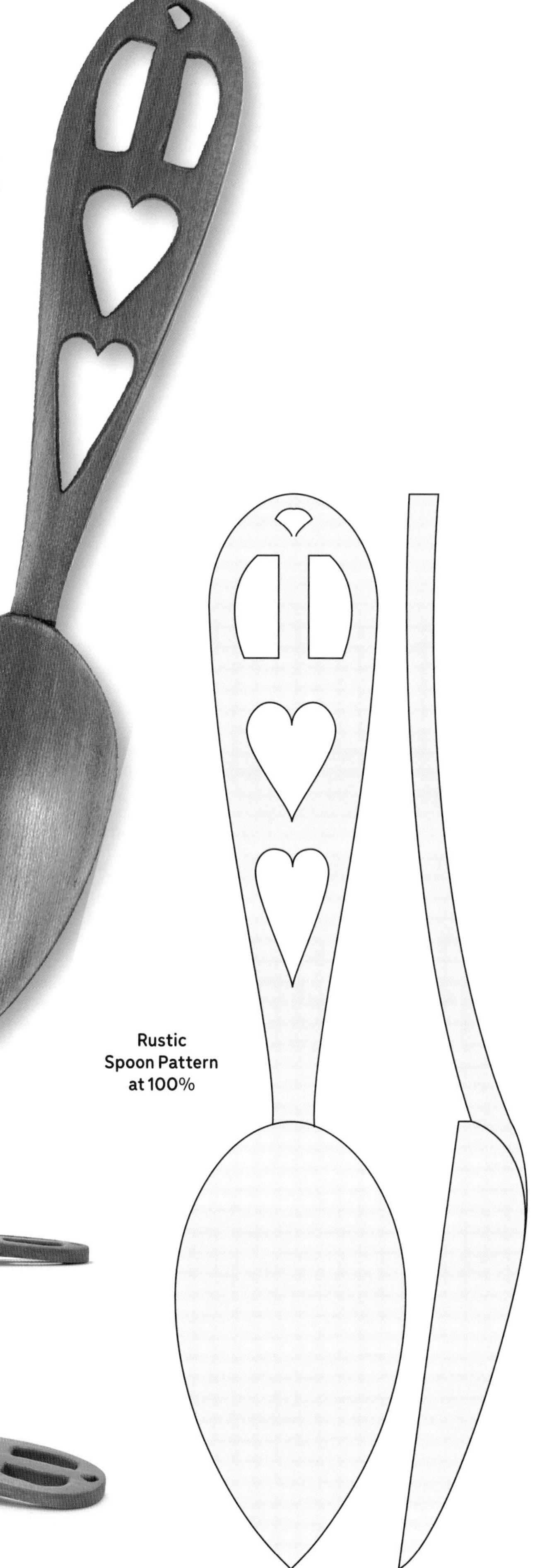

Rustic Spoon Pattern at 100%

Bywyd (Life) Spoon

This design utilizes basic chip-carved bordering combined with a simple fretted heart detail at the crown to create an evocative result. The spacious fretted areas, united with the luminous wood, give this spoon a light and airy feel.

Although there is a vague cross or ankh impression to the pattern, this is more by accident than by design. Crosses and religious imagery were almost unheard of on historical Welsh lovespoons, which is curious given how devout the majority of the country was during the spoon's heyday. The cross pattern simply adds a bit of structural support in this heavily fretted area of the design.

You will need to lay out the chip border carefully to ensure symmetry across the spoon. If you are not using a pattern directly fastened to the workpiece, make sure to take your time when drawing out the chip patterns to ensure equal numbers from side to side and that everything lines up as it should.

You can cut the fretted areas with a scroll saw or drill them out with a hand drill or press. You can also cut them away directly with a straight knife—this would be the more historically accurate (and time consuming) method of carving the spoon. This spoon has been carved from a very thin piece of wood, which further enhances the extremely delicate look and feel of the design, but which requires additional vigilance while carving to avoid breakages.

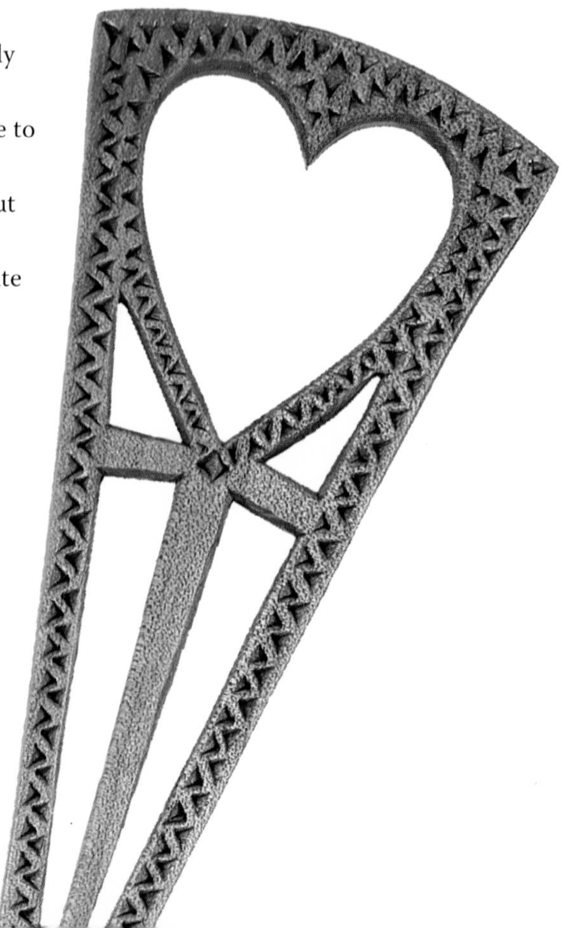

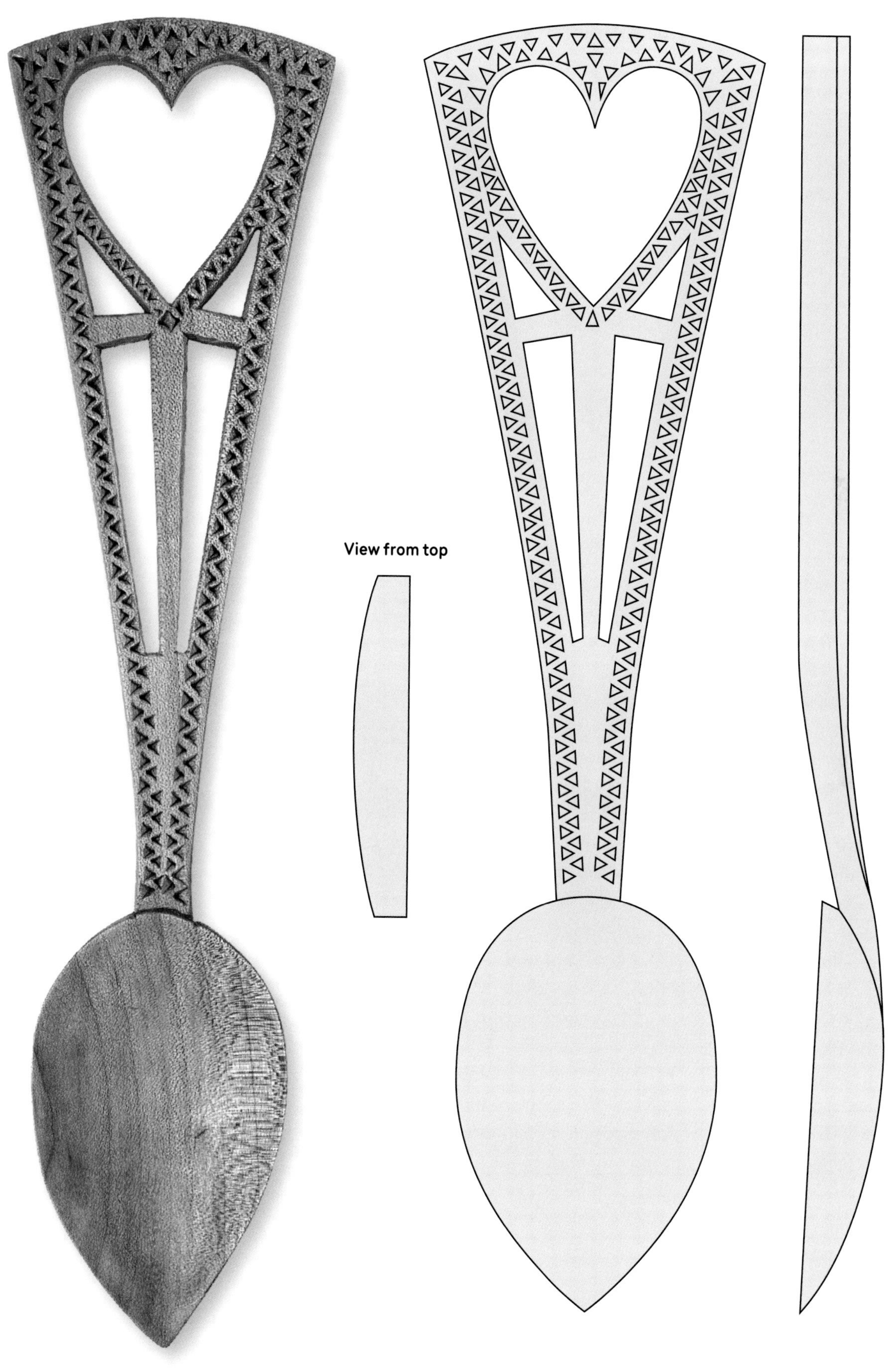

Bywyd (Life) Spoon Pattern
at 100%

Nola's Lovespoon

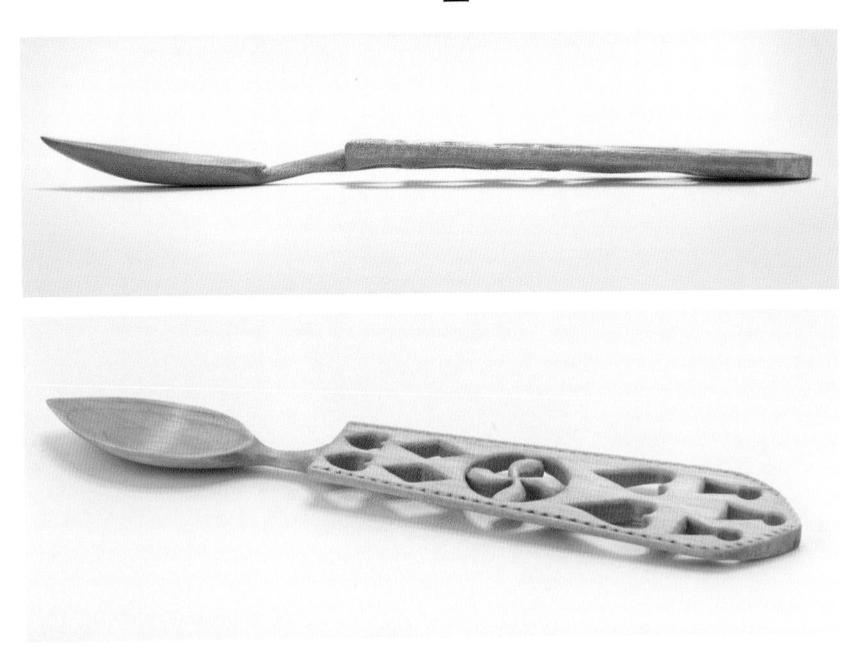

Simple but delightfully evocative, this small spoon utilizes basic symbols to create a complex love message. This spoon represents the type of design and messaging for which Welsh lovespoons have become justifiably famous.

Although dates, initials, and names are surprisingly rare on historical spoons, they are not entirely unknown. This design is shown both with and without simple initials. There were no rules to initialing a spoon; they could be first name, last name, both names, or variations thereof.

The love hearts and diamonds (a promise of prosperity) are presented in pairs to reinforce the idea of two joined together in love. The wheel of four comma-shaped "soul" symbols is an ancient pattern frequently found in European folk art, particularly that which originated in France and Germany. While the comma shape is now considered to be a symbol of the soul, its more likely origin is that of the raindrop, a symbol of fertility, growth, and plenty. The keyhole symbol is said to indicate either that the young lady holds the key to the young man's heart or that the young man will provide security.

The stems of the two spoons shown have been handled quite differently, resulting in very different looks. The rounded stem appears lighter and more delicate, while the squarer and more robust stem appears heavier. Choose the effect you want for your spoon.

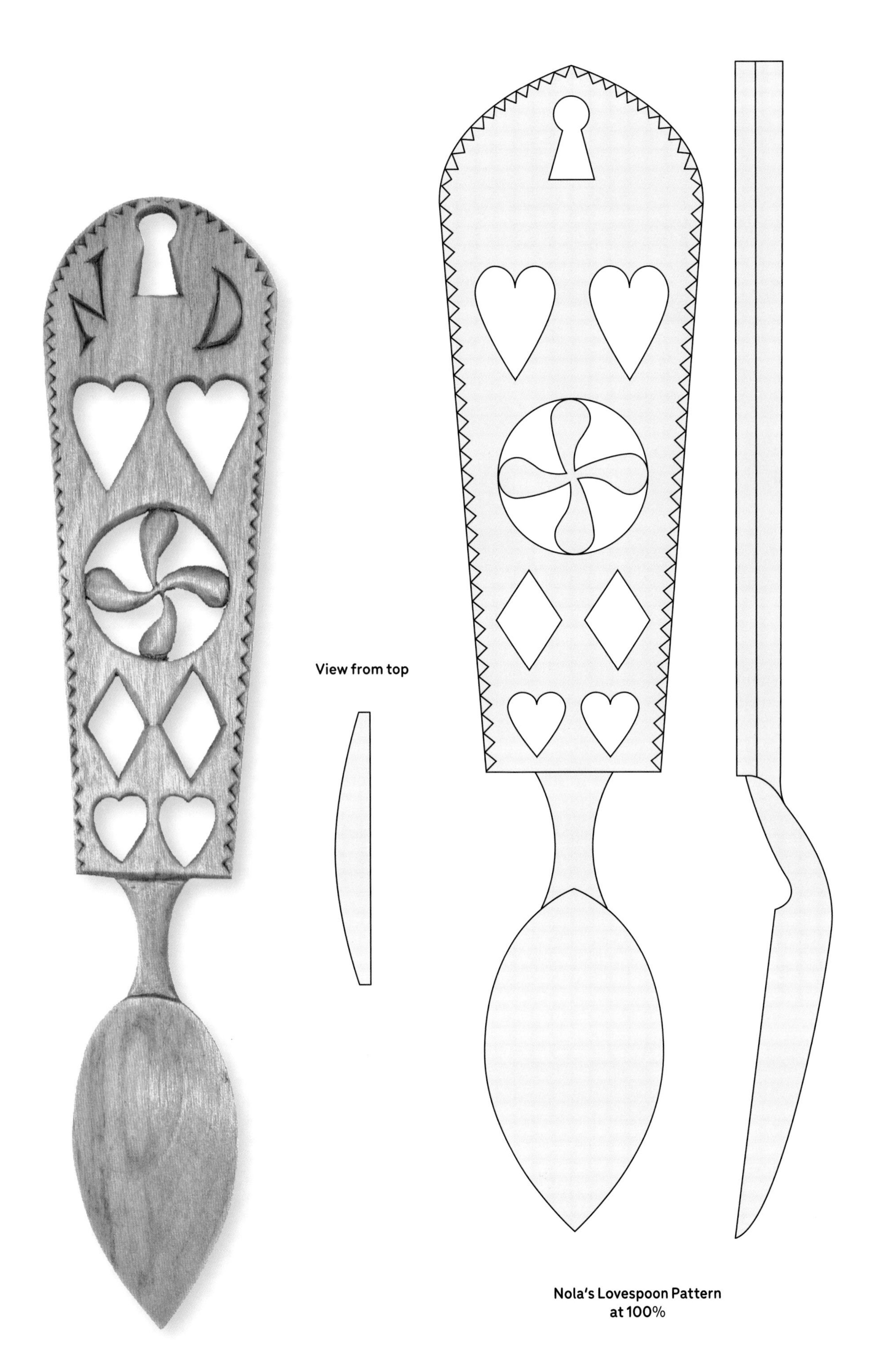
View from top
Nola's Lovespoon Pattern
at 100%

Rhodfa Fawr (Grand Avenue) Spoon

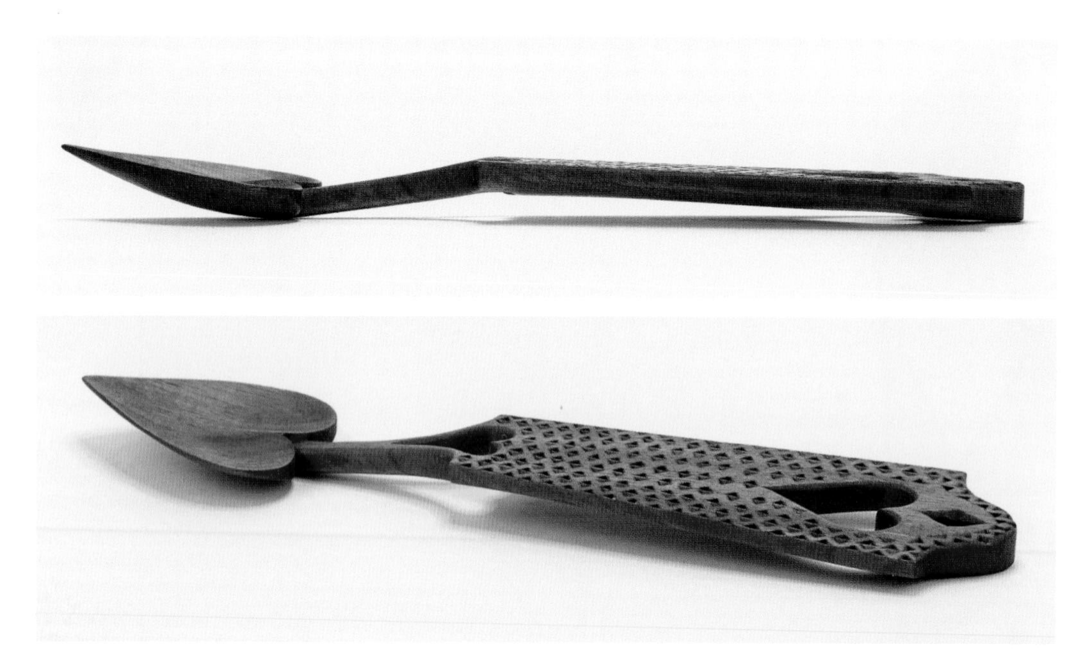

This simple but visually powerful pattern amply illustrates the way in which repetition of even the most elementary motif can result in a complex and sophisticated design. Here, rudimentary pairings of minimal triangular chip cuts that have been formed into several straight lines generate a unique and eye-catching design that is busy but remains ordered and restrained.

You will need a careful layout, a steady hand, and an exceptionally sharp knife in order to successfully carve this spoon. Consistency of size is crucial—if any of the triangles is larger or smaller than its neighbors, it will ruin the look of the entire design. Exercise great care and restraint with each cut!

Because of the fretted heart right at the spoon's stem, structural integrity is compromised in this area. It is easy to snap the spoon if you apply too much carving pressure, so be cautious. Keep a bit of extra thickness (from front to back rather than side to side) in this section to reduce the likelihood of a break.

The heart-shaped bowl appears occasionally in historical lovespoon carving, but it is more commonly used on modern spoons. Aside from looking terrific, it gives the carver the opportunity to show off nice wood figure and to symbolically suggest the idea of being fed by love.

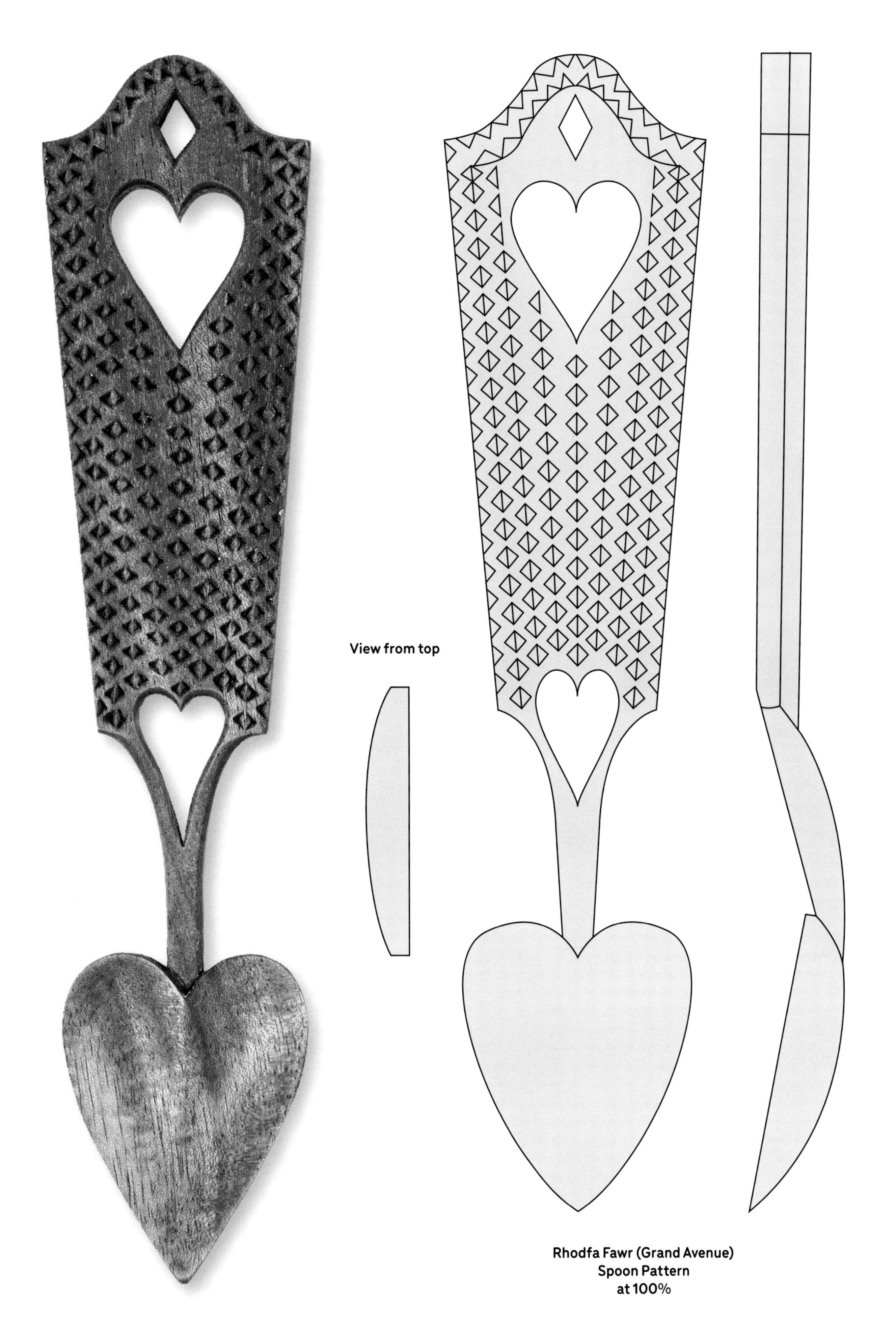

Rhodfa Fawr (Grand Avenue)
Spoon Pattern
at 100%

Menywod Cymru (Welsh Women) Spoons

Carvers have always been fond of trick carving, and it didn't take long until the famous ball-in-cage was being employed in Welsh lovespoon carving. In fact, the oldest dated Welsh spoon (1667) features a number of tiny balls carved into an elegant cage.

The first spoon design in this grouping is extremely straightforward and is an excellent first step for carvers new to the concept. The cage is square, with its width dependent on and equal with the thickness of the material available. It's vital that you carefully measure and lay out the cage and balls. The cage frame should be formed into a square with corners as close to 90 degrees as possible. Mistakes made at this stage will make accurate carving much more difficult later. The crown and stem of this spoon are approximately half (or slightly less) of the thickness of the cage and are cut down roughly one-quarter depth from both front and back faces. The stem should have a vigorous curve that should be drawn out before any stock is removed.

The second spoon is slightly more adventurous, retaining a square cage but adding more detailing on the stem and a nicely curved crown. The bowl should be shaped before thinning the stem to avoid the likelihood of breakage. The crown can be kept flat and straight for beginner carvers, but shaping a nice curve into it adds a bit more challenge and results in a more dynamic spoon.

The third spoon is the most complex version. The crown detail is especially dramatic, featuring an elegant fretted pattern of commas, a heart, and a fine decorative border detail. The crown is also sawn through the middle (from the side face) to create an unusual doubled feature. The cage bars are rounded and shaped like columns and are notable for the precise three-section finial and base.

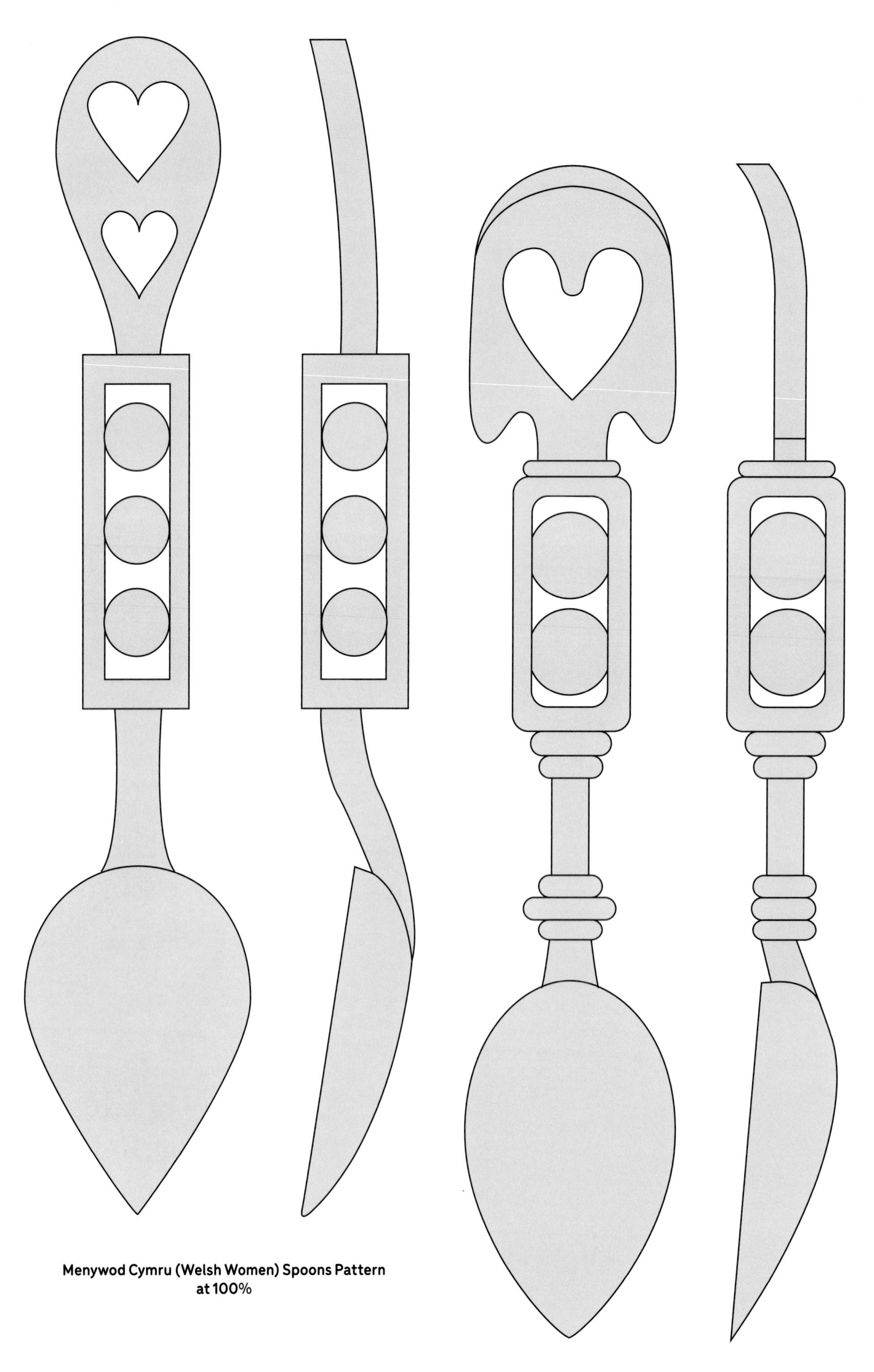

Menywod Cymru (Welsh Women) Spoons Pattern
at 100%

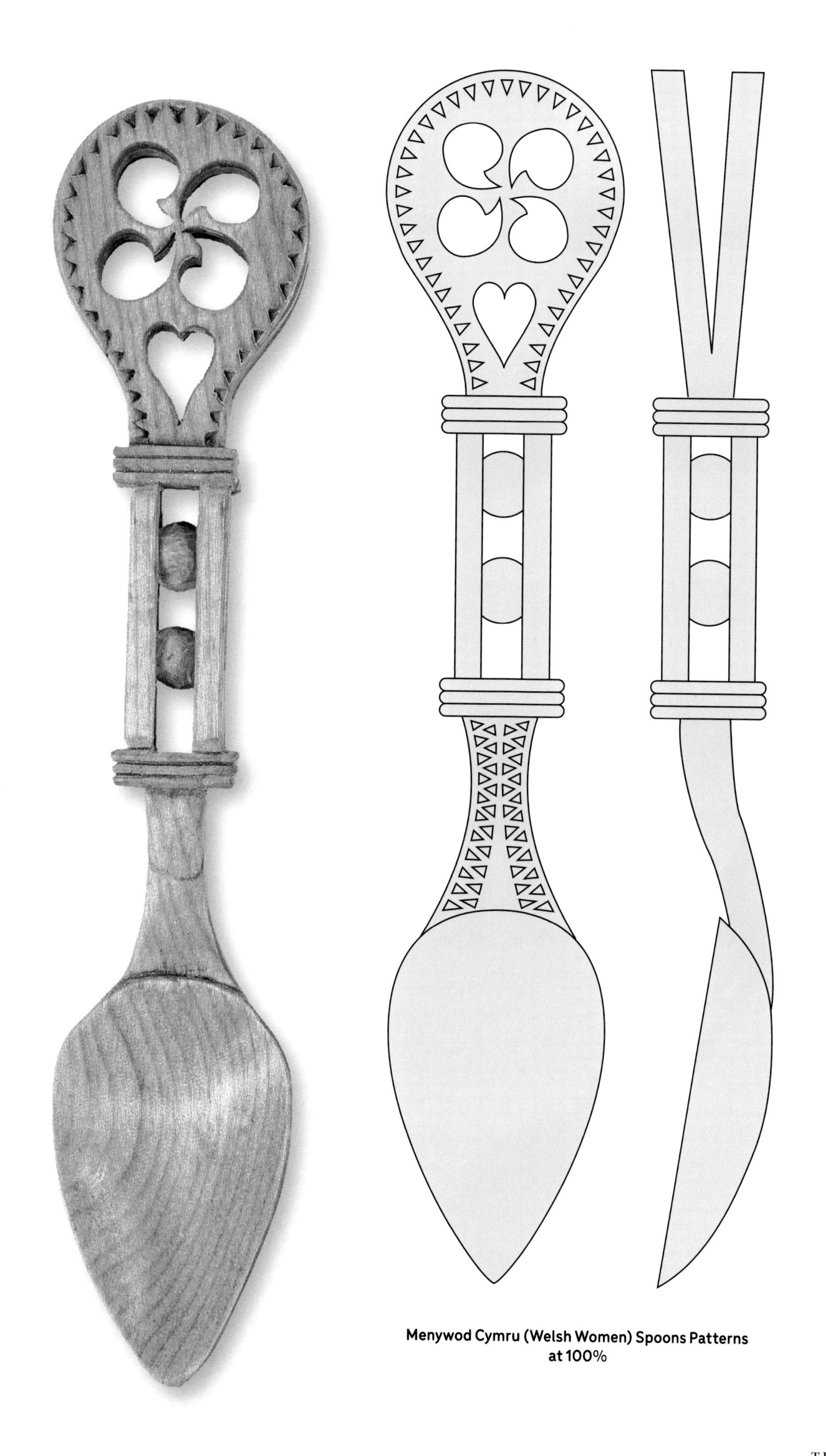

Menywod Cymru (Welsh Women) Spoons Patterns at 100%

Phyllis' Family Spoon

It didn't take long for famous carver's tricks, such as chain link and balls-in-cage, to become popular features of the Welsh lovespoon carver's arsenal. The balls may indicate a desire to have children, and the chain link may indicate the offer of protection or security. However, it's more likely that these symbolic attributions are the result of Victorian romanticizing rather than any conscious planning by early lovespoon carvers. Regardless, both the carving tricks and the mythology have now become part of lovespoon lore.

Carving the chain is a laborious process and requires beginning with a piece of timber as thick as the chain is to be wide. Take great care not to place undue stress on the thin links during shaping, as this could inadvertently snap them. The ball-in-cage is a bit less perilous to carve (unless the balls are carved too small or the cages too thin), but you still need a good deal of patience and hand skill.

This particular spoon is carved from walnut, but if you are a beginner, it may be easier for you to use a softer, more easily worked timber such as basswood, birch, or alder.

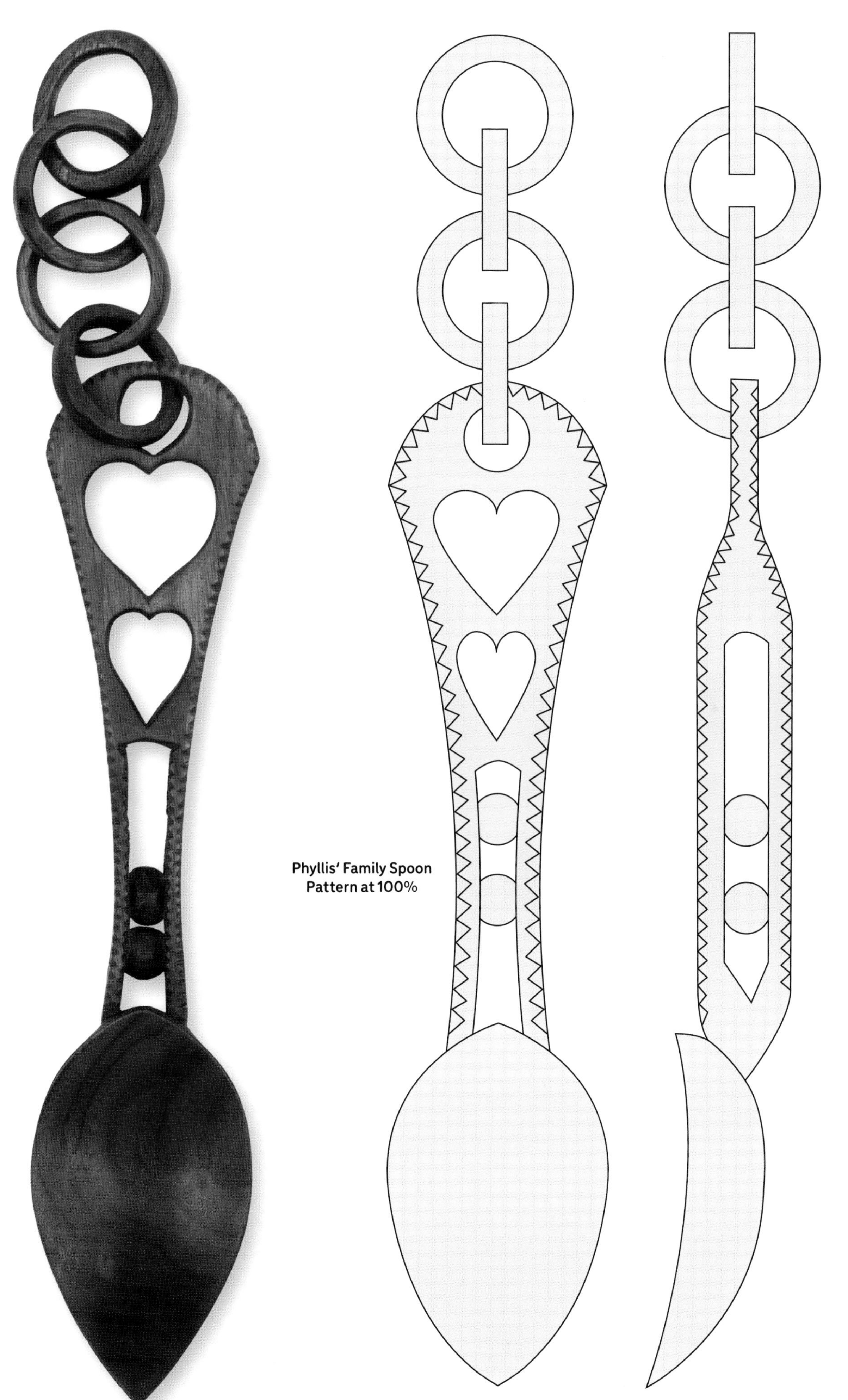

Phyllis' Family Spoon
Pattern at 100%

Morris Lovespoon

It's not known if the development of the panel style of Welsh lovespoon was the result of a need for more space to show off carving skills, but it has become the style of lovespoon carving most closely associated with Wales. Although heartily embraced by Welsh carvers (sometimes to an extreme), panel spoons also appeared in Scandinavia and, to a lesser extent, throughout Alpine and Southern Europe.

This particular design makes use of a pair of circular motifs and some fretted love hearts. The circle is a popular symbol throughout Europe; many circular patterns appear on romantic carvings from spoons to milking stools. As a circle has no beginning or end, it is the perfect symbol for eternity or the notion of eternal love. Circular patterns are also easily made with a rudimentary compass or even with a pin and short length of string.

In the absence of a compass or string, circular objects like bottle caps, lids, short lengths of pipe, or rings can be pressed into service to lay out circular patterns. The patterns are best fretted out with a saw, but you can also hand cut them with a knife or even leave them solid and relief carved. The fretted heart at the stem is a beautiful feature but takes a toll on the structural strength of the stem area. If you lack confidence in carving delicate, breakable areas like this, consider leaving the stem solid.

These two example spoons have been carved from white pine and pacific yew wood to demonstrate the effect that lighter-toned and darker-toned woods can have on a particular design.

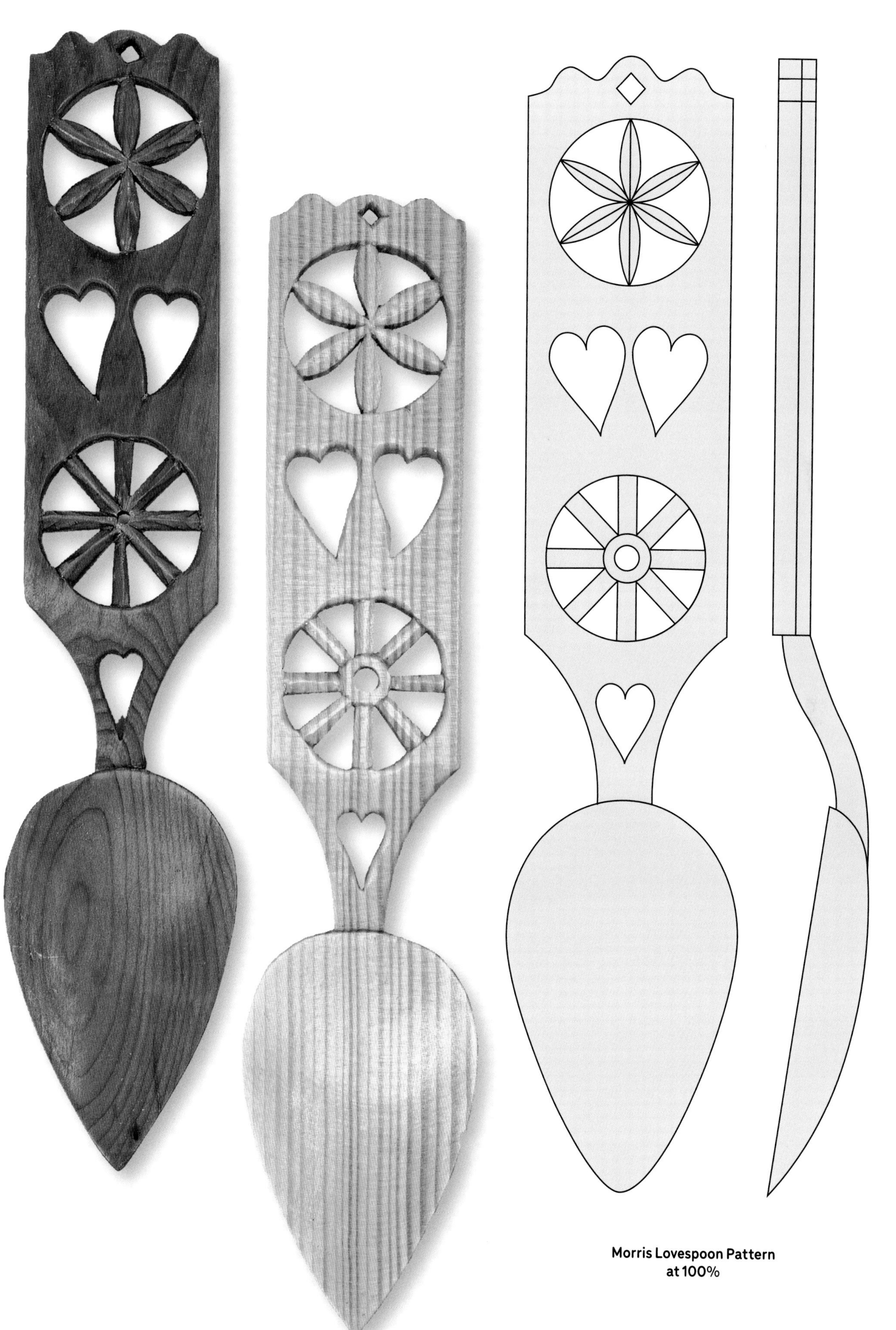

Morris Lovespoon Pattern at 100%

Gwyneth Lovespoon

This lovely, broad panel spoon takes advantage of a vigorous, sweeping taper to create a vibrant and exceptional panel handle. With its unique shape and the dramatic upside-down heart at the crown, the spoon is traditional but still feels vivaciously modern.

The exaggerated egg-shaped bowl continues the tapering theme and enhances the flow of the handle and stem, but you must take care not to make it too large or too small, or the effect will be lost.

The six-point flower motif has been further enhanced with love hearts. A pair of fretted commas and fretted hearts adds even more romantic symbolism. The border is a complex double line of triangular chip cutouts that form a nice herringbone zigzag.

The upside-down heart serves as a focal finish at the top of the spoon while also acting as a convenient place from which to hang the spoon for display on a wall.

You can carve this design with the handle kept flat, but doming it from side to side and top to stem will make it much more impressive. Hollow a complementary concave curve on the back to give the handle both a lighter appearance and feel. Leave some extra thickness at the back of the stem to lend structural support to a potentially weakened section of the carving.

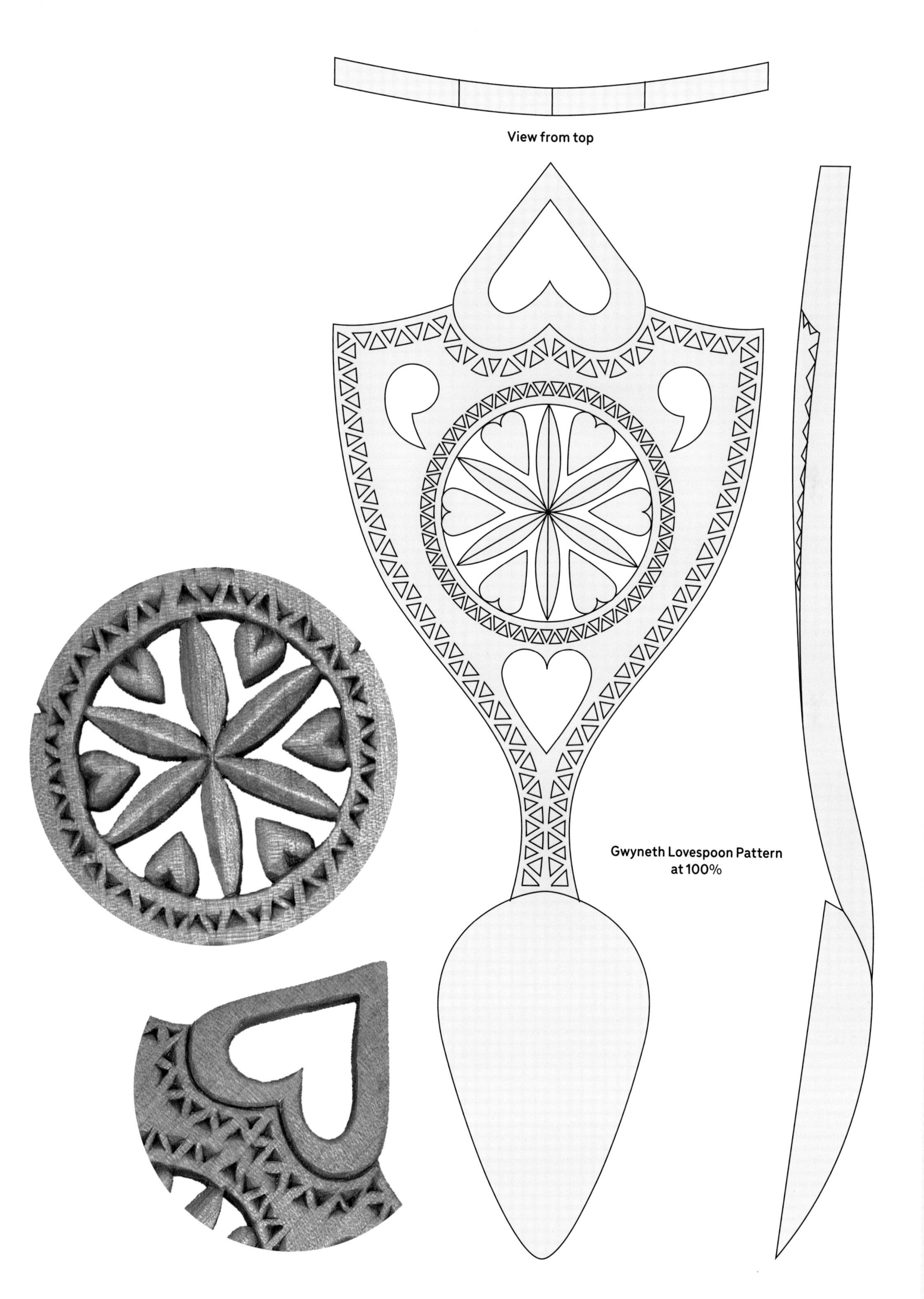
View from top
Gwyneth Lovespoon Pattern
at 100%

Cariad Mawr (Big Love) Spoon

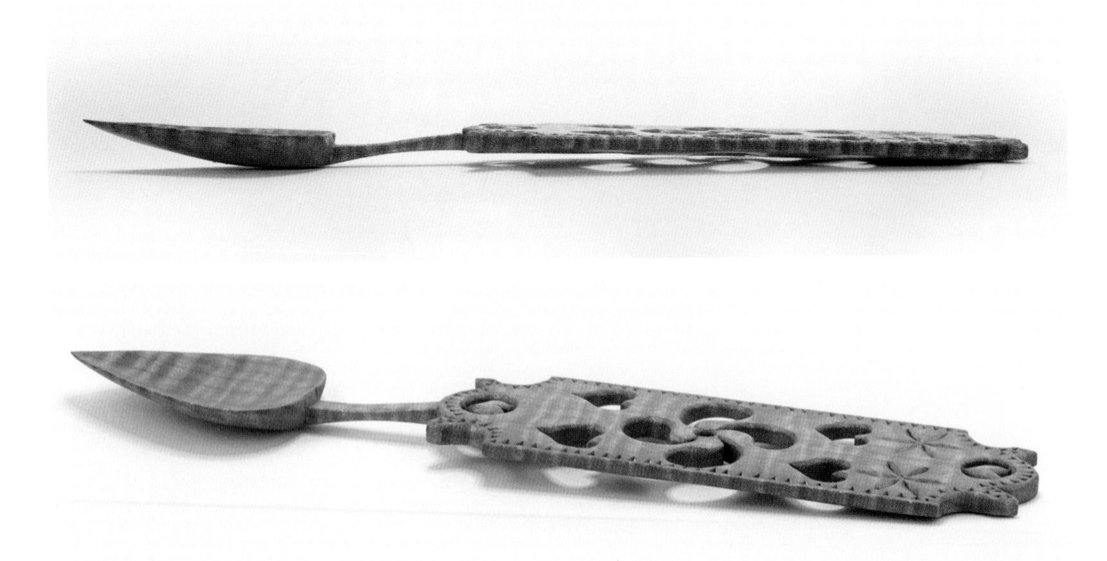

This long, broad, panel-style spoon has a wonderfully Victorian feel about it. Although it isn't a particularly difficult design, the stunning tiger-striped (or fiddleback) maple from which it is carved makes it gorgeous to look at and is evocative of a piece of fine furniture or an exquisite instrument. The shaped ends of the panel are typical of the ornate carving that marked romantic spoon carving through the mid- to late 1800s. The handle ornamentation is a tightrope-balancing act of busy detailing that has been restrained just enough so that the beauty of the maple is not lost.

Although the handle seems extremely thin when viewed from the side, it is actually about twice as thick in its center as at its crown. While the front face is flat, the back side has been rounded from a high center to low points at the outer edges. This makes the spoon feel exceptionally delicate while maintaining its structural strength.

Rather than simply fretting them, round and shape the hearts at the top and bottom of the handle into three-dimensional forms to make them much more eye-catching and refined.

You must exercise extreme caution during the carving of the exceptionally thin stem. The goal is to get it as narrow as possible, but with that comes a significant loss of structural strength and an increased risk of breakage.

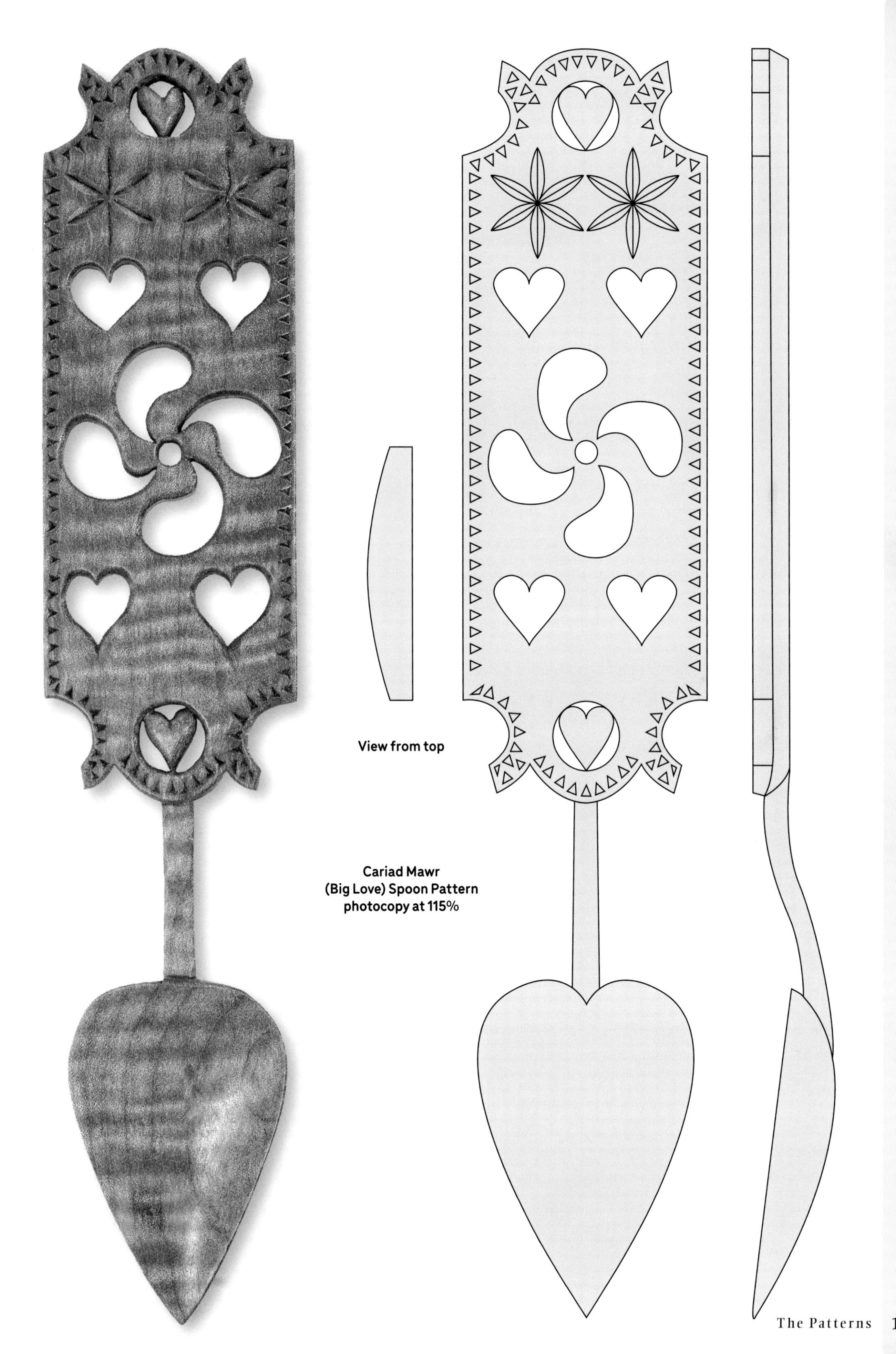

Cariad Mawr
(Big Love) Spoon Pattern
photocopy at 115%

Soul Drops Lovespoon

In the latter part of the 1800s, cheaper and more readily available tools such as jeweler's saws and treadle-powered scroll saws set off a craze for "gingerbread" work. From house fascia boards to cabinet fronts, flamboyantly fretted designs became ubiquitous. Lovespoons were no different, with ostentatious large panel spoons becoming extremely popular.

This design utilizes a number of popular fretted symbols—love hearts, prosperity diamonds, and wheels—to great effect. It also has a curious pattern that vaguely resembles a stained-glass church window frame. The meaning of this pattern is unknown, but it was popular enough that it appears on several antique spoons housed in Welsh museum collections.

As with the previous large panel spoon on page 136, this one has a flat face and a nicely rounded back. The stem has been left a bit thick to accommodate the steep sweep between the bowl and the handle, and the fairly large heart-shaped bowl shows off the wood's grain to good effect.

Undertake all the chip carving and detailing on the front face before carving the back down to size. If you shape the stem and back before completing the front detailing, you will have to cradle the spoon carefully while carving to avoid damage to the stem.

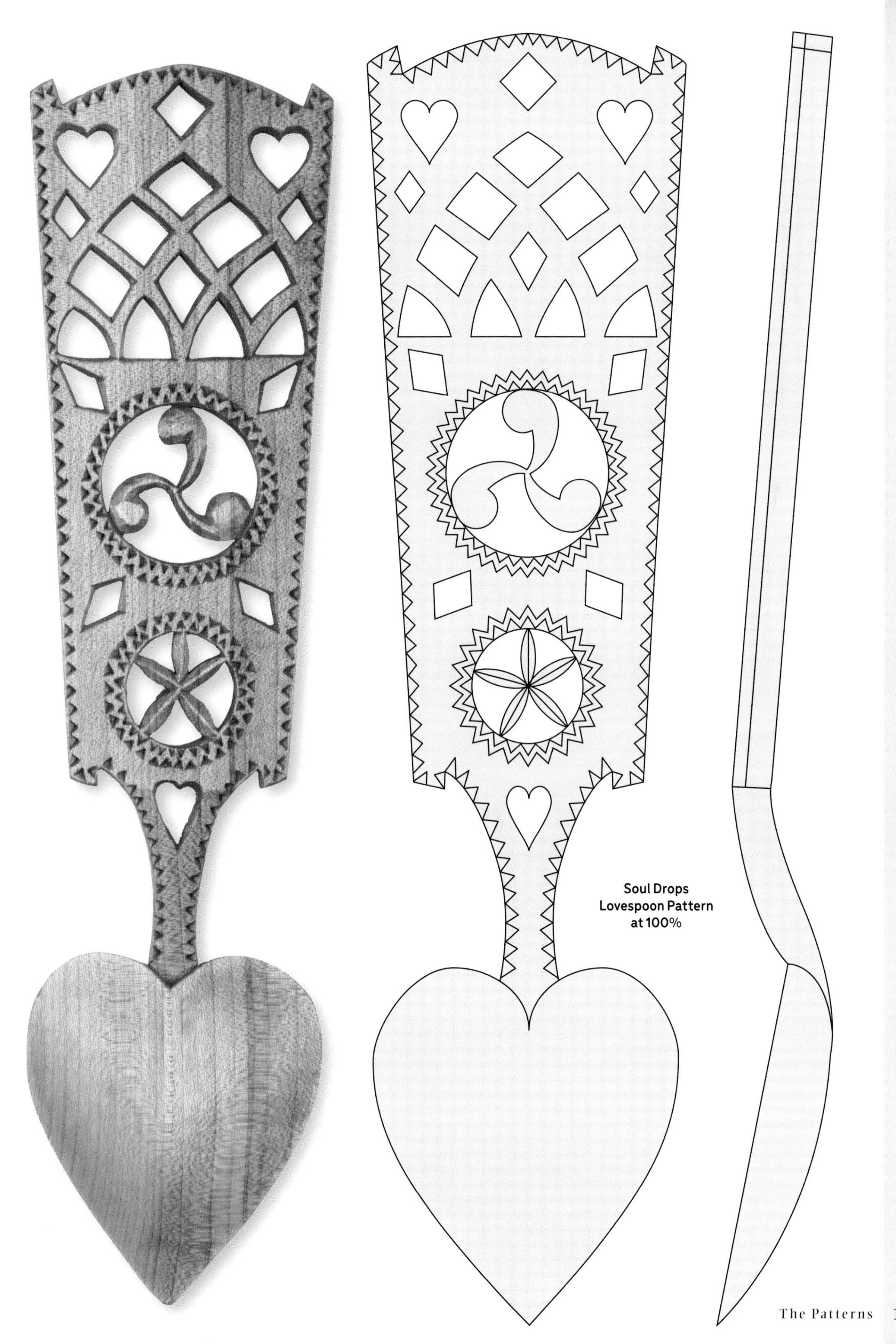
Soul Drops
Lovespoon Pattern
at 100%

Eternal Hearts Panel Spoon

This large, elegant panel spoon of mid-1800s design makes use of several of the best-known traditional lovespoon symbols. It is a large spoon typical of the period; many such spoons were so extensively fretted they became almost lacelike, but this particular design retains enough solid timber to have a bit of heft.

As with the previous large panel spoons (on pages 136 and 138), the front of the handle has been kept flat with the back of the panel having a gentle curve and thin edge.

The herringbone border is crisply carved and carefully laid out to encompass the entire frame. The border motif is also repeated around the central circular pattern of the design.

The stem is quite long and is gracefully curved, which makes it a little bit of a weak spot if not handled carefully. If you leave the stem thin, it will appear more elegant but will be structurally compromised. If you make it a bit thicker, it will lose some of its elegance but regain a fair bit of strength. Deciding how far to push things is a matter of experience and bravery.

Although they can be left flat and unadorned, the six-point flower and its accompanying hearts will look better if you shape, round over, and carefully finish them.

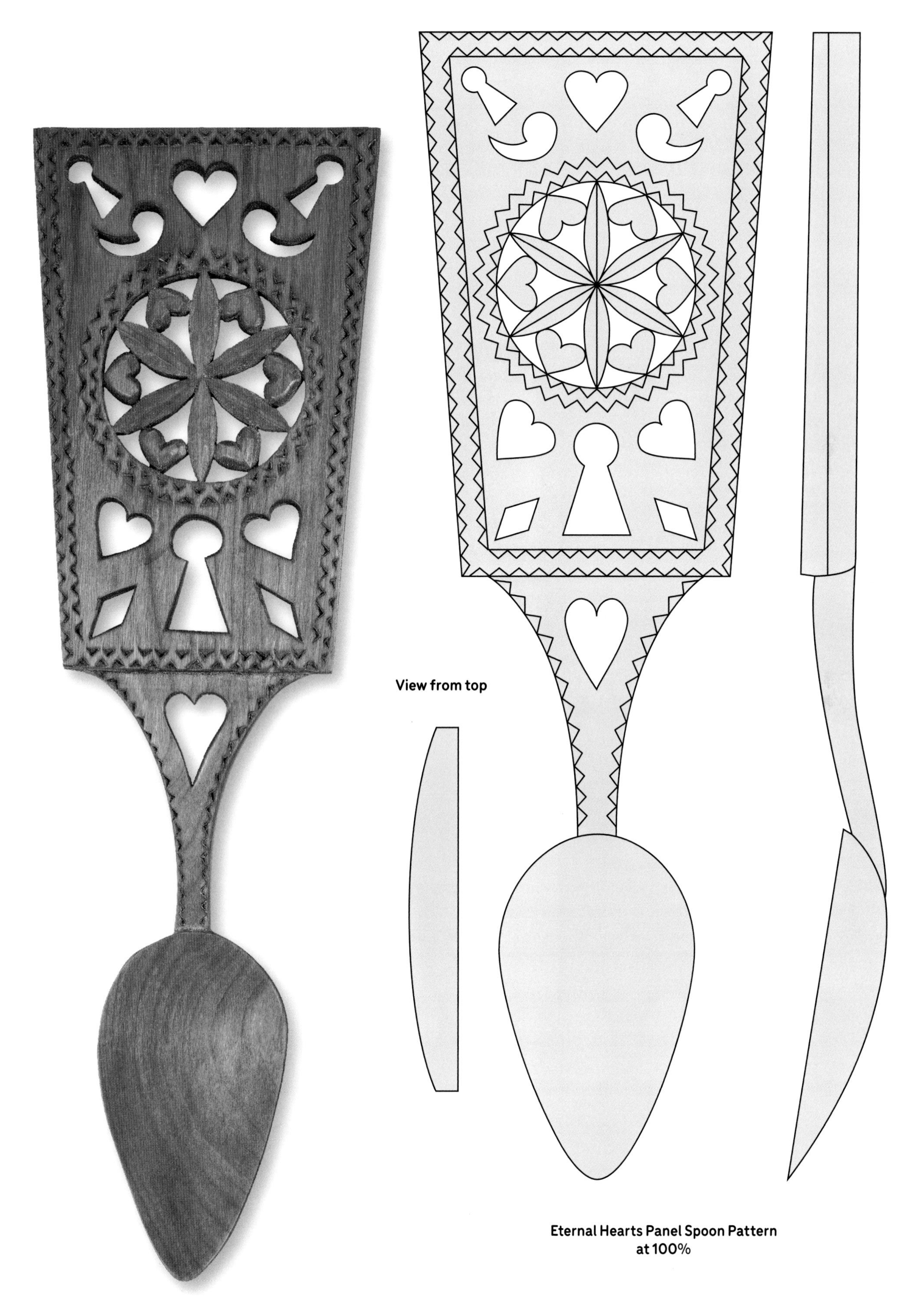

Eternal Hearts Panel Spoon Pattern at 100%

Resources

Romantic spoons can be found in a number of exceptional museum collections throughout Northern Europe. Many museums also have extraordinary online collections that allow the study of their holdings from virtually anywhere in the world.

St Fagans National Museum of History
St Fagans, Cardiff, Wales CF5 6XB
www.museum.wales/stfagans

Skansen
Djurgardsslatten 49-51
Stockholm, Sweden
www.skansen.se
info@skansen.se

Nordiska Museet
Djurgårdsvägen 6-16, 115 93
Stockholm, Sweden
Box 27820
www.nordiskamuseet.se
nordiska@nordiskamuseet.se

Norsk Folkemuseum
10 Bygdøy, Oslo, Norway
www.norskfolkemuseum.no
post@norskfolkemuseum.no

Tiroler Volkskunstmuseum
Universitätsstraße 2, 6020
Innsbruck, Austria
www.tiroler-landesmuseen.at
info@tiroler-landesmuseen.at

Bolzano Municipal Museum
Sparkassenstraße 14, Bozen
(Bolzano), Italy
www.gemeinde.bozen.it/stadtmuseum
stadtmuseum@gemeinde.bozen.it

The Breton Museum
1, rue du Roi Gradlon, 29000
Quimper, France
http://musee-breton.finistere.fr
musee.breton@cg29.fr

About the Author

Born in Wales, David Western now resides in British Columbia. He has dedicated the last 20 years of his life to carving decorative spoons and bringing the centuries-old tradition of lovespoon carving to the masses through in-person classes, magazine articles, books, and online educational resources. A regular contributor to *Woodcarving Illustrated* magazine and *Woodcarving* magazine (the latter being a publication of GMC, Europe's leading woodworking publisher), Dave has authored two prior Fox Chapel books on the subject of spoons—*Fine Art of Carving Lovespoons* and *History of Lovespoons*. He also hand-carves stunning commissioned pieces through his website, *www.davidwesternlovespoons.com*.

Fine Art of Carving Lovespoons
ISBN 978-1-56523-374-4

History of Lovespoons
ISBN 978-1-56523-673-8

Acknowledgments

Very special thanks to the all the fabulous museum curators and staff who have helped me with my spoon research over the years. A huge thanks to Dr. Herbert Roese, who opened my eyes to the vast and unexplored world of romantic spoon carving and who constantly challenged my assumptions and encouraged me to dig ever deeper into this fascinating subject. Deepest thanks of all to Nola, Charles, and Phyllis Western, without whom I would have never had the support and encouragement that enabled me to spend the time and effort required for a project like this.

Index

Note: Page numbers in *italics* indicate patterns.

Acanthus Spoon, *66–67*
alder (red) wood, 12
Alpine patterns
  about, 30; woods often used, 12
  Elegant Panel Spoon, *36–37*
  Herder's Spoon, *31*
  Jewelry Box Panel Spoon, *32–33*
  Tirolean Courting Spoon, *34–35*
  Wedding Spoon, *38–39*
axe/adze, 13–14

ball-in-cage motif, 26, 27, *126–29*, *130–31*
band saw, 14
bent/hook knife, 13
bigleaf maple wood, 12
birch wood, 12
bowl of spoon, 10, 24, 25
Breton-style spoons
  about, 25, 40; woods for, 12
  Breton Flowers Spoon, *45–46*
  Breton Geometric Pattern Spoon, *47–48*
  Breton Six-Point Star Spoon, *49*
  Folding Spoon, *50–51*
  Simple Breton Spoons, *41–44*
Bywyd (Life) Spoon, *120–21*

Cariad Mawr (Big Love) Spoon, *136–37*
carving spoons
  about: romantic spoon carving, 8
  arch shaping, illustrated, 11
  basic cuts, 16
  customizing your spoons, 24–25
  motifs and symbols guide, 26–27
  parts of a spoon and, 9–11
  safety, 17
  step-by-step guide, 18–23
  tools for, 13–14
  woods for, 12
cherry wood, 12
Chip-Carved Heart Spoons, *116–18*
circular patterns, about, 26
clovers, four-leaf, 26
Continental spoons, 25, 26
cuts, basic, 16
Cwtch Bach (Little Cuddle) Spoon, *110–11*

"Danish oil" style finish, 15
diamonds
  about, 26, 27
  patterns with, *32–33*, *79–81*, *98–99*, *110–11*, *122–23*, *138–39*
Double Hearts Spoon, *54–55*
drill press, 14

Eastern maple wood, 12
Elegant Panel Spoon, *36–37*
Eternal Hearts Panel Spoon, *140–41*

fans. *See also* Jewelry Box Panel Spoon
  about: step-by-step carving guide, 18–23
  Fan Spoon, *60–61*
  Heart and Fan Spoon, *86–87*
  Heart Spoons, *90–92*
  Knotwork Spoons, *100–102*
  Pocket Tester Spoons, *79–81*
files, 14
film finishes, 15
finishing spoons, 15
Floral Heart Spoon, *64–65*
Flowing Spoons, *93–94*
Folding Spoon, *50–51*
Four Hearts Spoon, *58–59*
Four-Heart Courting Spoons, *82–85*
four-leaf clovers, symbolism of, 26
Fretted Shield Spoon, *98–99*

goals of this book, 9
gouges, 14
Gwyneth Lovespoon, *134–35*

handles, 9, 24–25
Heart and Fan Spoon, *86–87*
hearts. *See also* Welsh spoons
  about: symbolism meanings, 26; wheel with, illustrated, 27
  Double Hearts Spoon, *54–55*
  Elegant Panel Spoon, *36–37*
  Fan Spoon, *60–61*
  Floral Heart Spoon, *64–65*
  Flowing Spoons, *93–94*
  Folding Spoon, *50–51*
  Four Hearts Spoon, *58–59*
  Four-Heart Courting Spoons, *82–85*
  Fretted Shield Spoon, *98–99*
  Heart and Fan Spoon, *86–87*
  Heart Spoons, *90–92*
  Jewelry Box Panel Spoon, *32–33*
  Long Hearts Spoons, *75–76*
  Notched Handle Spoon, *53*
  Pinwheel Hearts Spoon, *88–89*
  Pocket Tester Spoons, *79–81*
  Simple Breton Spoons, *41–44*
  Simple Passion Spoon, *103–4*
  Simple Tester Spoons, *73–74*
  Stylized Hearts Spoon, *56–57*
  Triple Crown Spoon, *77–78*
  Wedding Blocks Spoon, *68–69*
  Wedding Spoon, *38–39*
Herder's Spoon, *31*
hook knife, 13

Jewelry Box Panel Spoon, *32–33*

keys and keyholes, 26, 27, *122–23*
knives, 13–14
Knotwork Spoons, *100–102*

Long Hearts Spoons, *75–76*

maple woods, 12
Menywod Cymru (Welsh Women) Spoons, *126–29*
Morris Lovespoon, *132–33*
motifs and symbols guide, 26–27

Nola's Lovespoon, *122–23*
Norwegian spoons
  about, 52
  Acanthus Spoon, *66–67*
  Chain Wedding Spoons, *70–71*
  Double Hearts Spoon, *54–55*
  Fan Spoon, *60–61*
  Floral Heart Spoon, *64–65*
  Four Hearts Spoon, *58–59*
  Notched Handle Spoon, *53*
  Spoon Rack Display Spoon, *62–63*
  Stylized Hearts Spoon, *56–57*
  Wedding Blocks Spoon, *68–69*
Notched Handle Spoon, *53*

oil, finishing wood with, 15

paring cut, 16
Patterns, overview of, 28–29
penetrating oil, 15
Phyllis' Family Spoon, *130–31*
pine wood, 12
Pinwheel Hearts Spoon, *88–89*
Pinwheel Spoon, *96–97*
Pocket Tester Spoons, *79–81*
poplar wood, 12
push cut, 16

raindrops, symbolism of, 26
red alder wood, 12
Rhodfa Fawr (Grand Avenue) Spoon, *124–25*
Roese Spoon, *114–15*
romantic spoon carving, about, 8, 26–27. *See also* carving spoons
Rustic Spoon, *119*

safety, 17
saws, 14
Scandinavian style, 25. *See also* Norwegian spoons; Swedish spoons
scrapers, 14
scroll saw, 14
sharpening stones/papers, 14
shield, fretted, *98–99*
Simple Breton Spoons, *41–44*
Simple Passion Spoon, *103–4*
Simple Tester Spoons, *73–74*
Soul Drops Lovespoon, *138–39*
Spoon Rack Display Spoon, *62–63*
spoons. *See also* carving spoons
  about: goals of this book, 9
  back sides, 11
  bowls of, 10
  finishing, 15
  handles, 9
  stems, 10
  woods for, 12
stems, about, 10
step-by-step carving guide, 18–23
stop cut, 16
straight knife, 13
Stylized Hearts Spoon, *56–57*
Swedish spoons
  about, 72
  Flowing Spoons, *93–94*
  Four-Heart Courting Spoons, *82–85*
  Fretted Shield Spoon, *98–99*
  Heart and Fan Spoon, *86–87*
  Heart Spoons, *90–92*
  Knotwork Spoons, *100–102*
  Long Hearts Spoons, *75–76*
  Pinwheel Hearts Spoon, *88–89*
  Pinwheel Spoon, *96–97*
  Pocket Tester Spoons, *79–81*
  Rings of Love Spoon, *105–106*
  Simple Passion Spoon, *103–4*
  Simple Tester Spoons, *73–74*
  Triple Crown Spoon, *77–78*
  Wedding Rings Spoon, *107–108*
symbols and motifs guide, 26–27

Tirolean Courting Spoon, *34–35*
tools, 13–14
Triple Crown Spoon, *77–78*

vines, symbolism of, 26
V-shaped cut, 16

Wedding Blocks Spoon, *68–69*
Wedding Spoon, *38–39*
Welsh spoons
  about, 72, 109; customizing, 25; examples illustrated, 8, 9
  Bywyd (Life) Spoon, *120–21*
  Cariad Mawr (Big Love) Spoon, *136–37*
  Chip-Carved Heart Spoons, *116–18*
  Cwtch Bach (Little Cuddle) Spoon, *110–11*
  Eternal Hearts Panel Spoon, *140–41*
  Gwyneth Lovespoon, *134–35*
  Menywod Cymru (Welsh Women) Spoons, *126–29*
  Morris Lovespoon, *132–33*
  Nola's Lovespoon, *122–23*
  Phyllis' Family Spoon, *130–31*
  Rhodfa Fawr (Grand Avenue) Spoon, *124–25*
  Roese Spoon, *114–15*
  Rustic Spoon, *119*
  Soul Drops Lovespoon, *138–39*
  Y Llwyau Metel (The Metal Spoons), *112–13*
wheels of fortune, 26, 27
woods for spoons, 12

Y Llwyau Metel (The Metal Spoons), *112–13*

A Badger's Tale

Naturewatch Foundation Edition

From the Nature's Heroes series

by

Geoff Francis

First published in Great Britain in 2019 by No More Dodos
www.nomoredodos.org

Words by Geoff Francis

ISBN 978-1-907729-37-9

Thanks to Jennie Rudd, Andy Swinburne, Claire Brazington, Melissa Ramplin and Jacky Francis Walker

Edited by Jacky Francis Walker
Designed by Paul Windridge

Cover and interior: The illustrations included here are provided by the winners of the Naturewatch Foundation Badger Drawing Competition for entrants between 13 to 16 years old.

Cover image by Elita (age 13)

A Badger's Tale

Naturewatch Foundation Edition

From the Nature's Heroes series

Chapter 1

It was the first of May. The light behind the badly hung curtains was grey. Despite the lateness of the morning hour, it did little to illuminate the chaos in the room. Liam's tired eyes lazily focused on the haversack, which sat at the foot of the bunk ladder. The drawers and cupboards, such as they were, had been ransacked in great haste. Jackets, shirts, jeans and shoes, which would not be suitable to be inherited by his younger brother, had been pushed and prodded into one big pile in the centre of the room. Liam began to make his choice from amongst them. Whatever would fit into the rucksack he was going to take.

Today was Liam's birthday. Today he was ten years old and today he was leaving home. Where was not important, just that he went. It was the way of things in this house. Michael, his older brother, had gone and Seamus, who was now six, would have to leave when it was his turn. Today it was Liam's.

Just like her newly dyed hair, Angie's heart was an unnatural shade of black. In a desperate attempt to make her life somehow stable, conventional and strangely normal she regularly tried to jettison her past. Her intention was to take on a new persona to go with a new man in her life. Each one of the boys' fathers arrived at such a time and so, in due course, did each of the boys, her sons.

Ten was a good age. That was when Angie's mother had left her. Today Liam was ten and it was his turn. He closed the door and forced the key back through the letterbox as was his habit. He always followed his mother's instructions to the letter.

Chapter 2

The haversack felt heavy on his back. It was disproportionately large against his small fry frame as he made his way along the street. He had no idea where he was going to go. Children's voices echoed from the park, so he followed them. Laughter, tears, screams, anguish and abuse mingled as mothers and children confronted each other in the half-term playground. He watched from a distance, sitting astride his rucksack. There was no reason or thing to draw him near. He recognised one of the shrieking mothers. She was a friend of Angie; that is, they signed on at the same job centre on the same day. She probably wouldn't have known him for she never appeared to be interested in anything but herself.

He tucked himself under the ground-trailing branches of a fir tree just to be sure he couldn't be seen. It was a place he would often take sanctuary. He propped himself against his bag and spied on the world from his secret hide. Gradually he began to doze, then would wake, uncertain of where or why he was in this place. But the reasons soon returned. One time, as he drifted out of his temporary sleep, he heard a man's voice. "Didn't I see you girls with a lovely, big, fierce-looking dog?"

Leeona (age 13)

Liam looked up to see a man in his thirties with two girls about the same age as Liam. The trio were standing not ten feet away on the grass in front of him.

"Morag isn't fierce. She's lovely!" exclaimed one of the girls.

"I'm not sure about that," said the man. "You'd need to prove it to me."

Her friend began to tug at her cardigan. "We must go home, we will be late for tea."

"I tell you what, you come back this evening without your friend, and you can show me your dog then."

The girls ran off. The man looked around. Liam froze but he hadn't been spotted. The man waited a while and then walked purposefully away, grinning.

When the girls reached home, their roles reversed. The one who had been so quiet suddenly found her voice. She told of the man and the things he had said to her friend. Once her mother was satisfied in the truth of her story, she went to the phone.

Chapter 3

Liam lay in the twilight, uncertain whether it was safer to stay or go. He heard movement close by. There were muffled voices. He strained his eyes to see if it was the little girl who had come back. He was aware that there was another person a little bit further away. But meanwhile someone else was getting very much closer. Whoever it was, they were nearly on him. He thought he heard a radio burst sharply and briefly into life.

Perhaps someone had reported him as being missing. But whoever would? No one was bothered. An owl hooted and startled him. Involuntarily, he shifted tightly into his rucksack for comfort. What light there was, was blocked by a large figure looking down at him. It was the man from the afternoon.

The figure was abruptly jerked backwards by two sets of powerful arms in the darkness and forced to the ground. The man's face turned towards Liam. His eyes were looking straight into Liam's hiding place.
The distorted face grinned straight at him. Then the man was hoisted bodily off the ground and frog-marched into the night.

A police radio crackled through the gathering darkness.

"Yes Jim, it was the bloke you thought."

Abbie (age 14)

“Let’s hope his dognapping days are curtailed for a while,” commented a fresh-faced bobby.

The reply came in a strong, reassured, but world-weary voice with a North Country accent.

“The problem is, son, even when they get to court, the sentences they get given are too lenient. Often derisory. No deterrent to that sort of villain. The magistrates should get to see the true horror of what happens when they put the dogs to attack and kill badgers.”

“Badgers?” queried the young officer.

“No doubt that’s what he wanted the dog for. They like those powerful Staffie crosses, do the badger baiters. Patterdale terriers are another favourite.”

“My mum has a couple of rescued Staffies. They are the gentlest dogs I‘ve ever known. Love and licks on four slightly stiff legs.”

“You’re right son, and I had a Patterdale when I was growing up.”

“But not when those scum have finished with them.”

“That’s just criminal!”

“But that is what they are.”

They both smiled wryly, recognising the unintended pun.

“They will all have form - burglary, theft, drug dealing and more. I’ll wager that bloke we just caught has a record going back to teenage years… and further. Wouldn’t be surprised if his dad didn’t have one too.”

Chapter 4

Although sounds of the evening had long faded, the awful grin would not. Its haunting presence said to Liam he needed to leave that place. Having made the decision, he started to move quickly towards the perimeter fence of the park. He knew there was a hole where three railings were missing. All the kids knew about it.

Once through the fence, he walked without thinking, following his feet along the lamplit pavement trying to outpace that grin, which faded then loomed at the very front of his mind. The soft echo of his footsteps on

Catherine (age 13)

the concrete of the pavement turned to a fierce crunching sound, then softened to a crisp crackling of leaves underfoot. He stopped and shook himself out of his nightmarish reverie to find that in running from the darkness in his mind he had unwittingly brought himself to a place that was even darker, in a physical sense at least.

He was standing in a small clearing. Clouds hid the moon, and trees surrounded him menacingly. He turned to the left, right, right, left, left, right, left, right. The place began to swirl about him. 'Which way did he come in? Which way was out?' Everything looked the same - dark and frightening. He was lost and he knew it. Tears began to run from his eyes. But he didn't cry out. He was too afraid 'the grin' might hear. Liam collapsed upon his rucksack and held tight for whatever comfort it could give him. There he lay until exhaustion overtook the fear, and sleep found him for a while.

He was wakened by a snuffling sound close by. He held his eyes screwed shut, fearful that if he opened them he would encounter that terrible grinning mask again. But the sound didn't get any closer. It seemed to be remaining at the same distance. There was a confident shuffling amongst the leaves and, whatever creature it was, seemed to be indifferent to his own presence. Slowly, Liam unscrewed one eyelid. Through the darkness he caught a glimpse of white. 'It's a ghost,' he thought and simultaneously, irresistibly, totally out of his control, his other eyelid popped open.

Off to the left of where he lay was a creature about the size of a dog. Liam smiled. He liked dogs. It wasn't like any dog he had seen before though. It was very stocky and sturdily built with a distinctive grey and white coat. The hair appeared much coarser than any dog he had known and he didn't think he would enjoy stroking it. The animal was occupied with scratching at the ground with quite fearsome looking claws. It was rooting for something amongst the leaves. When it discovered what it was looking for, a strong muzzle completed the purpose of the search and something disappeared into the animal's mouth. Liam had never seen such a creature before. He watched with delight. All the other thoughts were banished. The animal clearly seemed comfortable in Liam's company, as it wasn't until a full half-hour had passed when it finally turned to examine the young human more closely.

Chapter 5

The animal set off into the darkness of the wood. Liam followed. At no time did Liam feel uncertain as to whether he should follow his four-footed guide. Despite the darkness, the further he went, the warmer and safer the forest felt. And the colder and more dangerous the world outside became. Clouds dispersed and uncovered the moon, which shone bright as sunlight revealing a new world. Deepening shadows created strange shapes to right and left. His ears were awakened to new sounds, but he didn't feel discomforted.

Sol (age 16)

The trees became less dense. Another clearing opened before him. At its centre a number of entrances had been excavated. The area was peopled by half a dozen creatures similar to his guide. The smaller ones were romping together in energetic play. They stopped and looked at Liam through their little eyes. Then they recommenced their interrupted games.

The one who had led him there looked back at him. Liam took this as an invitation - an instruction to stay. He dropped his rucksack to the ground, propped his head on it as a pillow and fell into the sweetest sleep to the comforting snuffling sounds of his new companions.

Each day, as he watched the badgers (for this is what the creatures were), he learned from them. He took particular note of the one who had led him there. Over time he gathered that she was something of a fierce 'boss lady'. He gave her the name Boudica after the legendary female leader of the early Britons. He had loved the tales of ancient times and tradition, which Angie would sometimes read to him to coax him into sleep.

Intuitively, Liam understood the badgers' need to be reclusive, keeping well clear of those of his own kind. In his short life, he had already had enough experience of their cold-hearted fickleness and disloyalty. The search for food forced him to go somewhat dangerously, but cautiously, close to human habitation. Here, the results of the excess and profligacy of people nearly always provided a multitudinous choice of diet. He was amazed and delighted to discover what had been discarded by individuals and shops. The bins at the rear of supermarkets were the richest pickings, and he would always eat royally following a visit there. He made his forays in the darkest part of the night.

Chapter 6

Returning on one such night, he lost his way. Rather than exacerbate his situation, he settled in the undergrowth, drew some of his new won booty from his haversack, ate his fill and promptly fell asleep. He woke with the rising sun in his eyes. Before he could distinguish anything clearly, his nostrils were assailed by a bouquet of decay from a cage trap, sitting beside a hedge about five feet from the ground on top of a collection of stacked hay bales.

As the warmth reached the chilled corners of the trap, he saw that a large bird was held captive there. Initially, it appeared to be just black and white, then the iridescent richness of the bird's feathers responded to the light, and its fierce voice found a sad cry. A cry to reach beyond its confines. A cry to anyone who would hear. A life in mourning was as much expression as it would ever be allowed, day after day. Until one morning when her voice would no longer be. Liam heard its voice and understood that there was no way the bird could indulge its desire to explore the wonderful warmth, which at that moment quickened its body.

felt, with the air rushing wildly into her lungs.
'Do you want
tiara?'
'Not especially
'Do you
beginni
a song and you
'OK.'
So, as the
way round the
mountain
roads towards Katoomba and the air
became cooler,
Gemma played songs from an
ed tape collection.
After the first opening bars
outed out the names
of the songs and Gemma
ollies as prizes.
'I'm predicting a
she said and before
she'd even pressed
yelled, '"VENUS!"'
Bananarama's 'Ve
od I LOVE this song!'
from the year the
used to dance to it on
top of their
bly erotic, until their
pression on her face.
nd breathed in the
itch; Lyn dropped
at is it?', and then
eze, sneeze and
aking their way
eresting sight of
Tears of mirth
tissues, and Cat
d, 'We need our
ry to tell. They
found a house,

Sean (age 14)

Liam pushed forward through the undergrowth, casting his eyes right and left, then moved deliberately towards the trap. He scrutinised it closely. Apart from its prisoner, there was nothing in the cage. No food, no water, no shelter. And in a separate compartment lay the emaciated body of another bird. It was the stench of its decay which had alerted Liam's olfactory senses.

He was feeling tense but felt it must be nothing against the stress of this creature, robbed of the freedom of flight. As it frantically hopped from one side of its confinement to the other, Liam reached out and released the trap. The game keeper would never know what small mysterious hand had secretly released the bird. The bird leapt free with a grateful screech.

Startled, Liam went to grab the closest means of support, which was the cage itself. Boy and cage tumbled to the ground crushing the evil device. He picked himself up and bent slowly to lift the body of the bird who had died a prisoner there. He made a silent blessing as he laid its body onto the grass. Then he cursed the ones who had made the trap and curtailed its life. Then Liam stamped on the offending item with as much strength as his legs could muster and ran. To his exquisite surprise, for a few paces, the bird flew beside him then dropped to the ground. He gathered it into his arms and kept running. A sense of complete satisfaction embraced his whole being.

He knew that from this moment on, he would do whatever was within his power to save animals and birds from the cruelty of his own kind. He would be looking for whatever needed to be set free - in himself and in the world he shared.

Chapter 7

More than what his eyes told him, Liam intuitively understood that something was wrong as he had gathered up the bird. When they reached the badgers' sett and stopped running, Liam examined the bird more closely. Its flight feathers had been clipped.

He spoke to the bird, whose intelligent eyes watched him intensely.

"I guess you and I are going to have to be friends for a while, so I need to call you something."

Since he could now recognise that she was a magpie, Maggie seemed the obvious choice. The bird turned its head onto the side, examining him quizzically.

To Liam's eyes, freed from its captivity, the bird looked almost regal in immaculate black and white plumage with its green and blue gloss. An image so far from the prejudiced, loutish reputation it had been given by

24kg at £89.50 = 3.73p; Draperstow
producer; 24.5kg at £89.00 = 3.63p;
Claudy producer; 23.5kg at £89.50 =
3.81p; Ballycastle producer; 23kg at
townbutler farmer.
Several heifers sold from £1,100 to
£1,435 each.
Good quality heavy heifers sold
steadily from £190 to £218 per 100 ki-
los for 562k Limousin at £1,225 from a
Benburb farmer.
A Newtownbutler farmer sold a
666k Charolais at £1,415 £212.
farmer 248k,
farmer 290k,
farmer 324k, £700, £216.00 and Ne-
wry farmer 326k, £690, £212.00.
closed for
cattle sales
information.
€60 to €135
on Monday, Janu
on Thursday, Jan
a prosperous N

Paul (age 14)

gamekeeper propaganda. A slander conjured long ago, conveniently forged in hunting's black heart, which required the death of millions of purposely bred birds. All this to satisfy what some considered to be corrupted appetites and minds in the name of entertainment. To assist in this purpose Maggie, like thousands of her kind before her, had been incarcerated in that evil cage.

Throughout the world, magpies are generally looked upon as being harbingers of good fortune.

In Native American myth the Navaho, Blackfoot and Cheyenne see the magpie as an ally and helper of people with shamanic powers. This was certainly to prove to be so for Liam.

Chapter 8

As the light began to recede, Liam and Maggie were roaming in the gloaming of evening's onset. Close by, a young male badger foraged for worms. Liam decided to call him Alden - meaning old friend, since he had been the very first of the clan's cubs to overcome his natural cautiousness towards the strange human.

While perched on Liam's shoulder, Maggie suddenly became very animated. True to the meaning of the first part of her name, Maggie began chattering insistently, as if guiding Liam in a particular direction.

Gradually, a shape like a Japanese Zen gateway emerged in the failing light - two upright posts joined by a crossbeam. Maggie flew the short distance to the crossbeam and began hopping from side to side of the entrance. Liam could resist no longer. Eventually understanding her promptings, he went through the aperture.

Immediately, the strangest sensations seized his body. Every vestige of what he had been in his short life until now was stripped away as if each atom was rearranging itself. He had entered as a young human. What emerged was a badger of an equivalent age.

For Maggie it was no surprise. She danced atop the gateway in delight.

Although Alden's dim, compromised eyesight had witnessed everything that had gone on with his one-time human companion, his sense of smell told him there was a strange badger in his clan's territory. He was initially alarmed and ready for a fray as his territorial instincts heightened and came to the fore.

This signalled danger for the transformed Liam. All badgers, especially the males, can be fierce in defence of their territory, and the ensuing conflicts can lead to some serious injuries. However, something of Liam's human smell had survived his transition. It echoed close to the surface in Alden's olfactory memory and

Tara (age 14)

subdued his instinct to attack. After all, even as a human, Liam had become a strange adjunct to the clan, and badgers are fiercely loyal to their family. Soon, Liam and he were romping together in pure badger style. It seemed the most natural thing to do.

Liam was discovering and inhabiting his second nature. He wondered if any of his own kind had the potential to understand on that level.

Chapter 9

Following their romping games, the two young badgers returned to the sett.

When Liam entered the domed entrance he was not prepared for what he found within. He had entered a labyrinth, which would unfold over a thousand metres. Established more than a century before, it had been a place of safety for generations of badgers to retreat underground during the day, shelter from adverse weather conditions, raise their young, sleep, socialise with other clan members and keep warm during the winter.

The main sett was made up of many different chambers. Each chamber clearly had a different function. These were interlinked by a maze of tunnels with many active entrances.

Off the main sett, Liam eventually discovered subsidiary setts, where he found his friend, Boudica, and her three cubs; two females and one male. Despite her dominant position within the clan, she had chosen to nest there because it was much quieter. The cubs were, in human parlance, 'exceedingly cute'. Straight away, Liam's heart was captured by them as he watched them play and saw how they interacted with each other. To each he gave a name to reflect the characteristics he saw.

There was a magical mist enveloping the scene he witnessed. The names he chose to identify these visions of delight were drawn from stories which, just occasionally, had managed temporarily to bring a fleeting joy into his young life. The smallest he called Fae meaning fairy. She looked so fragile when he first saw her. Her sister seemed very concerned that their larger brother's rough male play should not inadvertently harm little Fae, so Liam called her Willa, the protector. The male cub seemed to have a sense of independence and magic about him. Liam named him Merlin after the magician, the helper and guide to King Arthur in the Legends of the Round Table tales, which had enchanted Liam's young imagination.

Throughout, Liam's human appetite remained. Often at night he returned to the gateway and became a boy again. He scavenged the bins but always took no more than he might need for several days. When his hunger was satisfied, he would take the uneaten food and stash it safely, close to the sett, but not too close, in order to avoid attracting unwelcome fellow scavengers.

Sasha (age 14)

Whilst Maggie remained his companion, on his way back he would collect any road kills he found for her to feast on. After seven months her feathers had finally grown back. She became agitated and clearly needed to leave.

In comparison to Liam, her life's span was likely to be a short one. In line with the rest of her species, it was possible it may be as little as two and a half years in all, probably no more than four years. As much time as was hers, she needed to live it. The debts each owed the other were cancelled out. He was sad to see her fly away but glad to see her healthy and free.

Chapter 10

The seasons passed. Summer to autumn to winter to spring.

Around the time of Liam's arrival at the sett, Boudica's cubs had begun to be more courageous and were exploring their surroundings.

Within four weeks, the cubs had been weaned. They foraged with Boudica and began to leave the sett before darkness arrived. This was especially true of Fae who had a very independent streak, despite being smaller than her two siblings, Merlin and Willa. All three cubs loved to play… Willa protecting Fae from the inevitable rough play of Merlin. Later, badger Liam and Alden were able to provide an occasional foil for the young male's games.

When the weather became dry, the cubs began to play less and eat more, going off to feed soon after emerging from the sett. When the weather was particularly dry, the prevailing conditions were especially harmful for the cubs. At times like these, Liam had seen the adults eating wheat and corn, even wasps' nests.

When the autumn came, the sows were ready to mate again. This was peak time for the collection of bedding and digging out the sett ready for winter. The badgers now had to put on weight as rapidly as possible, eating a wider variety of food, notably fruits and nuts.

As winter approached, food became harder to find. The badgers emerged from the sett later and later in the evening and needed to start relying on their fat reserves.

The badgers, whilst not hibernating, slept for longer and longer periods, emerging less often. At this time, even though mating had taken place long before in spring and autumn, the females only now became pregnant, their bodies having delayed the fertilisation of the eggs.

Edward (age 14)

The clan spent a lot of time in the relative warmth underground, and would intermittently go outside to feed, even when snow covered the ground.

Then, not long after the winter equinox, most of the cubs were born. Paradoxically, it was also the time when the next round of mating occurred.

The early signs of spring began to manifest. Disputes occurred amongst the males and a great many signs of territorial marking became obvious. The collection of fresh bedding was also a prominent activity after the long winter.

Later in that season, the clan started to come out of their setts before full darkness, and the cubs would emerge from their underground home for the first time.

And so it went. Seasons followed round again. And again.

For the clan, including Liam, life was not always easy. Half the cubs born sometimes did not survive the year, but for those who did, it was a relatively safe existence. It was better than the life Liam had come from. This was more of a home than the one he had been born into. He learned much from his adopted family. Their natural reclusive privacy matched his own. Yet they were warm and sociable within the sett. Their ferocious loyalty and courage when protecting themselves and each other was a quality he would always aspire to match.

Chapter 11

What Liam saw, his mind did not want to comprehend.

Devastation spread out before him.

In his past human existence, he had witnessed similar scenes briefly on TV, on news programmes and in films: Encampments annihilated by cavalry, napalmed communities totally devastated in combat, bulldozed and bullet-torn homes, and bloodied bodies of soldiers and families ravaged by war. All these he had seen and experienced second-hand in his earlier young life.

This was different. This was real. Too real!

This had been his home for thirteen seasons. A home he had shared with creatures he had come to love, whose unconditional compassion had stretched across the species barrier.

Ilaria (age 13)

Now, for all he knew, they were all dead or dying. What other conclusion could he reach? There was so much blood that Liam didn't think he would be able to identify anyone for certain.

Those who had done this had chosen the daytime, when they knew the badgers would be underground; and the spring, when nursing mothers would fight ferociously to defend her babies. Alden's mum, Boudica, had been nursing her new cubs when the spades broke through to her nursing chamber.

At a distance, Liam saw a group of men laughing together and taking selfies. Liam realised that what they held in their arms were the bloodied bodies of his 'family'. And they appeared so proud of what they had done.

As he stared, not wanting to believe what he saw, he recognised that one of the humans held the crumpled shredded corpses of little Fae and her brother, Merlin. Stretched between two others was the lifeless body of the great Boudica. She had fought so bravely that it gave the men a perverted source of pride and achievement to have killed her.

Now Boudica had been torn apart, and so had the clan where she had given life to so many. It was she who had led Liam to the sett. He had often wondered if it was the mother in her that had recognised the lost child in him. Whatever it was, he was overwhelmingly grateful to her.

Anger welled inside him. He knew that if he had been in his human form his guts would be spewing onto the ground. The last thing he wanted to be was human.

The men had joined other animals into their treacherous assault on the natural world. Beside them stood lurchers and small terriers, which had been sent down the sett armed with tracking equipment to locate the badgers. The men had dug down into the chambers where Liam and his friends had so often found warmth and safety from the outside world. They had dragged out the badgers and thrown them to the dogs. Judging by their appearance, two of the dogs had sustained horrible injuries. They were covered in mud and blood, and had open wounds to their legs and lower jaws.

With the disgust he felt for these men, Liam never wanted to go back into his human body again.

Suddenly, one of the men spotted him. "We missed one!" he shouted.

The human set off towards Liam wielding a spade. He called back to the others. "Keep hold of the dogs. This one is mine!"

Liam ran. He had to reach the gateway as fast as he could. It was his only chance.

Bismah (age 16)

Chapter 12

A badger can reach up to nineteen miles per hour but only over short distances. The gateway was at least a quarter of a mile away.

Happily, the man was encumbered by his wellington boots, which made this awkward creature even more cumbersome. In addition, the shovel was affecting his balance.

Nonetheless, after Liam's initial turn of speed the man seemed to be gaining on Liam with every step.

However, the man was overweight and his beer swilling habits were taking their toll, making him breathless with the exertion. He came to a full stop.

A younger fitter man grabbed the spade as if collecting a baton in a relay race. His pursuit was likely to be more efficacious.

The gateway was in sight. All Liam could do was hope. His short legs were in pain, exhausted from his pursuit as he ran as fast as he could.

He was in and through. He lay flat on the grass and rolled over, tucked his hands behind his head to stare as nonchalantly as he could at the sky, as if contemplating the heavens.

The man ran past the gateway. His head had been down, checking the rough ground to avoid stumbling, and had not witnessed the transition of badger to boy. He stopped stock still and surveyed the landscape. Spotting the boy, he shouted "Where did he go!!!?" Liam pretended confusion.

"The badger! The bloody badger!!"

Liam pointed to what he knew was the boggiest ground in the area.

The man did not stop to question what a young boy might be doing there. His blood was up and his bloodlust clouded every other thought he might have been able to conjure. It was questionable of course that he had ever been able to think.

Sounds can carry far in the quiet of the country. Some five minutes later, Liam heard a loud cursing as his would-be pursuer struggled to keep his green wellingtons attached to his feet. The bog was sucking him down.

Liam removed himself from the location quickly and discreetly.

Olivia (age 14)

Chapter 13

That evening Liam had no appetite, but to displace the pain he was feeling inside he had to do something.

He found himself in town mindlessly searching the food skips and dustbins, but he soon became tired of the task. His thoughts were constantly of his badger family and the horror he had witnessed. The tormented body of little Fae and the magical Merlin. It was clear that Boudica had matched the famous queen of ancient history and legend, after whom he had named her.

As he envisaged her bravery - how she must have fought ferociously to defend her new cubs and the rest of the clan, he was choked inside. A tear trickled from his eye. It was because they knew that a mother would defend her own that the baiters had chosen this time of year, and had so prized the torment and death of Boudica. She had certainly taken her toll on the dogs but that sort of human didn't care about that. They had a bloodlust and that was what they wanted to see - blood and plenty of pain.

Liam could not help but think of his own mother, Angie, and how she would have responded if he had been the victim of such an attack. He knew for certain in his heart she would not have lifted a finger.

In the seasons he had spent among the clan, he had come to understand how they all depended on each other's deeply rooted support. Even in the hardest, darkest winters, they had been comforted and bolstered not just by the physical warmth they brought to each other, but by a true sense of belonging.

He loved them and the life they shared, but now that was gone.

Normally, Liam was super cautious to keep out of sight and not be seen by anyone. But this evening he did not care. He was in deep despair. Suddenly he was overcome. He started to blubber uncontrollably. He dropped to the pavement, squatted on the kerb's edge and sobbed loudly. It was not long before he drew the attention of a policeman who was patrolling the area.

A voice that was distantly familiar broke in on Liam's pain. He looked up through tear-filled eyes. Had he been able to see more clearly he might just have been able to conjure the face of the young officer who had been part of the arrest of the man in the park when he first left home.

"What's wrong son? Has someone hurt you?"

"My friends. They have killed my friends. They've murdered my family."

The constable squatted beside him on the kerb. He was alarmed at what the boy had said but, cognisant of

Caleb (age 16)

his distress, he understood it might take some time to reach the nub of the matter. Gradually he was able to tease out the facts of what had happened and that his friends were in fact a group of badgers.

PC Durham, for that was the officer's name, was not just a community policeman. Like so many of his colleagues, he had voluntarily trained as a Wildlife Crime Officer so, to him, this sounded like a very serious crime.

"Can you take me to where this happened?"

Liam nodded. They got up and began to walk along the streets that would eventually reach the edge of the wood.

A group of men laughing and talking drunkenly loud approached. Liam shrank into the shadows. Sarcastically and arrogantly, one of them wished PC Durham a good night with a look that said, 'you won't get me', followed by a chilling unnerving grin. For different reasons, PC Durham and Liam recognised that grin.

Once the gang had passed, Liam said, "They're the ones."

"Which ones?"

"The ones who did it."

"Right son! Let's go and find the place."

As they walked, the PC, whom Liam was invited to call Andy, tried to prise details about Liam's parents from the boy with no success at all. When they reached the sett, the devastation somehow looked even more chilling when highlighted by torchlight.

The signs of badger digging had become all too familiar to Andy. The back filling of the holes they had dug to try and hide their actions was obvious. There was blood everywhere, from both badgers and dogs as Boudica, Fae and Merlin had fought ferociously for their lives. It was possible that the baiters themselves had also attacked the badgers using spades, clubs or knives. It was more than likely that the dogs had been injured themselves, and the injuries not treated by a vet in order to avoid detection of the day's activities, and the authorities alerted.

Andy told Liam that often the main evidence remaining at a badger crime scene is the sett digging, otherwise known as 'crowning down', and that without physical bodies being recovered, it was important to prove the sett had been in use by the badgers when it was attacked.

Sarah (age 13)

Andy added that if the badgers' bodies had not been hidden in the back-filled sett, they may have been placed at a roadside to imitate road kill. Andy feared these would be the most likely options in this case.

Chapter 14

PC Durham searched the area as best he could. He would return with his sergeant in the daylight to make a full report. There were no bodies. "They probably took them for trophies," he now told Liam, whose young soul chilled at the thought.

Andy continued, "With any luck, they'll be posting on social media, which will make them easier to identify. They take a perverted pride in what they do."

"I told you who it was!" anxiously interjected Liam.

"I understand. I believe you, don't think I don't. It's just we need something more, in fact, as much evidence as we can gather. How many bodies did you see?"

"There were three. Boudica, Fae and Merlin."

"What will have happened is that the other badgers will have dispersed and gone off to outlying setts. They have more than one."

This part of what Andy was saying Liam knew, of course, but he hadn't gone to search yet. What if he didn't find any others? What if his best friend, Alden, and young Willa were lost forever? It would have made everything feel so much worse. He knew that was an agony he couldn't yet face.

"Well, we had better get you home, son. Your mum will be worrying about you."

The irony of his words was not lost on Liam. This was his home and it had been devastated. He realised that, as sympathetic as the constable was, he would not understand and would be duty bound to return the boy to his human family, which of course did not exist, as far as Liam was concerned.

While the PC collected a final piece of evidence and his back was turned, Liam moved as silently as possible into the cover of the trees. He headed towards the gateway. Dutifully, the officer searched for the boy, but all he eventually spotted was a solitary badger. He smiled to see the creature, which he took for a survivor from the daylight slaughter.

Sinead (age 14)

Chapter 15

Wishing the darkness away. Waiting for the coming of the light to be announced in the throats of the birds. Back in human form, Liam sat staring into a pond located in the middle of the wood. When the breeze moved the waters, it was a place where he could watch the story of his badger clan play out before his eyes. He had spent many hours wrapped in wonder and delight. The latest episode, which was unfolding before him, held none of those qualities. His stomach churned, his fists were clenched in rage, and tears returned to his eyes. Within the image in the moving water, he saw Alden pulled away from the dogs by the baiters and thrown into a cage. Two of the men had then carried him away whilst Alden repeatedly hurled himself at the metal bars in a fit of fury and fear to escape his prison.

As the vision faded in the darkened muddy waters, Liam quickly returned to the devastated sett. He was hoping that Andy might just be there gathering more evidence, and happily for Liam, that proved to be the case.

But someone was with him, an older man with three stripes on his sleeve. At last, he heard the sergeant say, "Okay, I have seen as much as I need. Just finish off and I will see you back at the station in an hour".

As soon as Liam was certain the man was gone, he revealed himself.
"Where did you get to?" asked Andy.

"That's not important. They've taken Alden! They've taken one of them alive!"

"How do you know that?"

"Maybe I'll be able to tell you one day. For now, please believe me. They have! I don't know what they are going to do with him!"

"I do and it's not good."

Liam's stomach sank.

An hour later, back at the station Andy was talking to his sergeant.

"The word on the street is that they took a live badger for baiting."

"Who gave you this?"

Emily (age 14)

"The kid didn't want me to reveal who he was."

This wasn't quite the truth but it was better than admitting he did not know Liam's name.

"He also gave me an ID on the gang and they are known to us. One of their number was the guy we picked up in the park almost three years ago. He was trying to steal that little girl's Staffie cross."

The sergeant smiled.

"Well, he and his friends are worth a visit. Don't you agree?"

"I do indeed!"

Chapter 16

The two policemen were swift and unrelenting in their pursuit of evidence. Search warrants were executed at the mens' homes and their allotments searched.

At their homes, evidence revealed the dogs were owned by the baiters, and badger baiting equipment was found, including locators and hand-held tracking devices. Computers, lap tops and mobile phones were taken for forensic examination.

The men were arrested.

Visiting the mens' allotments, police seized spades, snares, smoking devices, implements to hold or kill badgers – gloves, tongs, sacks and nets, instruments, clubs, spades and knives. There in a pit they discovered Alden who was being held, awaiting a fight, which had been optimistically organised for two weeks hence. The badger was not in good shape, but heavy betting occurs at these events, often involving organised criminal gangs, so the men were determined to deliver him to them, even in poor shape. As far as they were concerned, it just meant the gangsters wouldn't need to cripple the badger in various ways as was the custom in these 'contests'. A healthy badger was more than a match for any single dog.

Andy and his sergeant had also found the dogs, which Liam had seen on the day of the baiters' attack on his home. One had serious injuries to its lower jaw. Another had injuries to its chest and the top of its legs.

The police took swabs from each dog's mouth and induced them to vomit, as well as taking samples of their faeces. They did this to retrieve badger hairs to prove that they had been in physical conflict within 24 to 48

Florrie (age 14)

hours previously.

DNA comparisons from the badger hair were made to scientifically prove it was badger hair beyond any doubt. Then DNA comparisons were made with the blood and dog fur found at the sett, with that of the seized dogs and retrieved badger hair. This was to link the dogs, and therefore the men, to the crime scene.

Chapter 17

Hidden in the shadows at the rear of a well-known supermarket, PC Andy Durham was loitering with intent. On his evening patrols he had noticed Liam's occasional visits to the food skips. He was very well aware that at least 35% of food was thrown away in Britain and consequently, although perhaps technically he might have been required to, he never moved to interfere with anyone who was going to make use of what would otherwise be wasted. He was hoping that this would be one of those evenings when Liam would be one of the beneficiaries of the throwaway society.

Andy and his sergeant had managed to retrieve the badger, which the baiters had taken alive. They had found it a place at a local wildlife sanctuary, however the animal was in a very sorry state and did not appear to have the will to survive.

Although the sanctuary insisted that they were not going to give up on trying to save its life, to Andy's surprise they were coming under pressure to put it down. He did not want to see this happen. He remembered how Liam had described the badgers as his family and Andy's intuition told him that, if he could just get the boy close to the ailing animal, there was a chance that its life force might return. However, he had to do this without anyone, particularly his sergeant, knowing, except, of course, the sanctuary owner.

Andy had waited a long time in the cold and was beginning to feel a certain degree of dereliction of duty. He had just decided he would wait another 10 minutes before having to move on, when Liam appeared.

Liam was delighted to hear the news that Alden was alive but bereft to be told that he was in such a bad way. Of course he would go - and straight away! Andy had to wait until the end of his shift but that was only an hour away. He told Liam to wait where he was and that he would pick him up in his car at 2:00 am. He knew that the people who run small sanctuaries generally are so dedicated to the animals they serve that it is nothing for them to be up all night and go without sleep for a number of days. So there was no problem for them when the off-duty policeman and young boy arrived at their gate at 2:45 am.

Liam was shocked, hurt and angry to see what had happened to his friend.

Sofia (age 15)

To the owner's surprise, and slight alarm, Liam opened the door to the cage in which Alden lay on a bed of straw. He stroked the precious head that he loved so much and put his hand in front of Alden's nose to let his friend smell and recognise his scent. Slowly Alden raised his head and focused his tiny eyes on his human brother.

Andy recognised the magical connection between the two, which excluded everything else that surrounded them. Everyone sat in silence for a long time, Liam stroking his brother's muzzle and tormented body. Alden rested safe in the reassurance of his brother's presence. It was only when Andy felt that Alden's healing had begun that he broke in on their enchanted kinship.

"'It was so lucky that we found him in time. The intelligence was that he was to be sold to a gang in London the very next day." A bitter smile crossed Liam's face. A mixture of joy and fierce anger.

Chapter 18

The results of the DNA forensic tests were conclusive in helping to prove a case against the men. As did the examination of their computers, lap tops and mobile phones, which revealed incriminating evidence of their participation in badger baiting, communication with co-offenders, and their keen interest in blood sports.

As Andy had told Liam, these people take a perverted pleasure in parading their cruelty - perhaps in some desperate exhibition of heartless machismo. Cameras, mobiles, sim cards, videos, maps and entries in personal diaries revealed just what they had done, barely credibly hiding their depravity by referring to the badgers as Pigs, Stripies, Billies, or Newcastle Supporters.

Summonsed to a Magistrates Court, the gang inevitably put in a 'not guilty' plea and the trial date was set for some months ahead. They were represented by one of a few defence lawyers who travel the country specialising in this type of crime. Both Liam and, more so, Andy, wondered how people could represent such evil men, defending the indefensible for a fiscal reward.

The case was heard by a District Judge who handed down the maximum sentence of six months and banned each member of the gang from keeping animals.

Grace (age 14)

Chapter 19

Liam searched every outlying and auxiliary sett but all he found were foxes or rabbits who were using them as temporary homes. Even in his sadness, the thought that they were providing shelter to other creatures brought a smile to his lips.

The other members of the clan had clearly dispersed to other areas and would have tried to integrate into different clans.

Then one evening as he sat forlorn at the main sett, Willa appeared.

She had been taken to a local wildlife rescue centre where they had carefully treated her wounds. She had just been returned to the wild.

Liam was ecstatic to see her, and she seemed very pleased to recognise him, even in his human form. They sat close to each other just waiting for the darkness to come. Animal and human seemed to understand the bond that defined their reliance on each other for survival.

In that moment, Liam recognised it was an understanding that needed to be universal. In order that they will survive, human beings need to cherish the natural world in all its diversity. Yet, in the remnants of their one-time home that lay before them, he saw the wantonly cruel destruction wrought by his own kind, and had to wonder if there was any chance for the things he loved.

He reached out his hand to stroke Willa's rough hair. And she allowed it. As he did so there was a familiar snuffling sound. Willa's nostrils responded immediately. She moved swiftly into the darkness where the sound was coming from.

Liam's heart sank. He wondered if his touch might have scared her away. He did not move to catch up with her, instead he remained where he was, desperately alone and quite bereft.

After about five minutes there was a crunching in the undergrowth. He imagined it sounded like two badgers coming his way. Willa emerged first and behind, from the shadows, came the familiar bustling form of Alden. His best friend had survived and was fit and free! Relief and elation flooded Liam's whole being.

The only thing to do now was for Liam to get to the gateway as soon as possible. Some badger style romping was in order!

Isabel (age 13)

Chapter 20

Liam found it hard to believe when Andy told him of the paltry sentence the men had received.

"They were my friends! The most they ever did was eat other animals to feed themselves. Not torture them for pleasure!" He was angry and close to tears of frustration.

"The ones they killed, my family, were innocent! Those men were guilty of murder and all they get is six months!"

"I know what you're feeling, believe me," said Andy. "We need to get wildlife crime recognised for what it is, a crime against life. At least baiters are now getting a lot of prison time rather than the community service orders they used to receive. If that is any comfort?"

"No, it isn't. How could it be?"

"Look - what you have brought us has been a fantastic help. I don't know how you get the insights you do, but they are priceless. Keep them coming."

Andy was duty bound to try to get Liam to tell him more about who he was. The only response he could elicit was "just for now you can call me 'BB'", said with a huge grin. It was a cheeky grin fit to melt any heart.

Andy looked at him confused. "BB?"

"For now it can be Badger Boy. Whoever knows what I'll be tomorrow."

"Ok, Badger Boy. I expect we'll be seeing you again?"

A reprise of the smile was Liam's silent reply.

Matt (age 14)

Natural Facts

Badgers

Badgers are a common species found worldwide. The European badger (Latin name Meles meles) is widespread across the UK, and is loved by most but seen by few due to their nocturnal nature.

European badgers have short stocky bodies, short tails, extremely strong jaws, short powerful legs and five powerful strong claws on their front feet. They grow up to 75cm from head to tail, and can weigh up to 12kg.

Badgers are easily recognisable due to their unique black and white striped faces, and their bodies have a soft undercoat of black fur with coarser grey and silver guard hair on top. Albino, ginger and dark European badgers do exist also, but they're very rare.

Badgers' eyes and ears are small, which is why they use their sense of smell to learn friend from foe, to communicate with other badgers, locate territories, hunt and forage. It is believed their sense of smell is 750 times stronger than a human's.

Male European badgers are called boars, females are sows and young badgers are cubs. Collectively they're called clans, and live in underground setts in groups of between two to twenty badgers.

Badgers belong to the same family as otters, polecats, ferrets, mink, stoats, weasels, pine martens and wolverines, which all have musk-bearing glands under their tails.

The badger mortality rate is high. This is due to road traffic accidents; habitat destruction; badger baiting and other forms of crime; and, in more recent years, the legalised badger cull.

Badger behaviour

Badgers are active both at twilight and during the night, and their behaviour differs from clan to clan.

Each badger clan has their own territory close to their main sett, which they defend fiercely. However, badgers do venture further afield into an area known as a home range, which contains secondary setts and regular feeding areas.

Home range areas and territories vary in size depending on food availability, local habitats and landscapes, and badger populations. Male badgers in particular will patrol their territories every night by walking regular pathways, scent marking and defecating in latrines. Badgers defecate and urinate in latrines that adjoining clans share to mark the boundaries of their territories.

Fights can happen should a badger venture into another clan's territory; boars in particular are fiercely territorial. Boars from neighbouring clans can be perceived as a threat as they may be seeking receptive sows. Badger fights usually result in nasty injuries due to their powerful claws, jaws, and sharp teeth.

Clans have a strict hierarchy that is dominated by a single boar. This boar will control all females for breeding purposes, though there will be a dominant breeding female. Young boars will attempt to climb the hierarchy to become the dominant male but this usually results in them being expelled from the clan.

All badgers carry a difference scent. Their musk is released from a gland under their tails, which badgers rub on each other to create a scent that is unique to their clan. This musk is also used to mark territories and trails.

Badgers can run for short periods of time, reaching 19 miles per hour.

Diet

Badgers prefer to forage for food alone despite living communally.

Their diet consists mainly of earthworms, slugs and other insects, however they have also been known to eat fruit, vegetables, nuts and grains, all of which they locate with their strong sense of smell.

Badgers are too slow to hunt other animals, but have occasionally dug up small mammal and amphibian nests to eat their young, and they will eat a dead animal carcass should they come across one.

Badgers don't hibernate, but they remain underground for longer periods of time in the winter and rely on their fat reserves. To prepare for this, they eat as much as they can in autumn, eating a huge variety of foods.

Setts

Depending on factors such as the abundance of food, clans can contain on average between two to twenty individuals, sharing a centrally located burrow system or 'sett', which is a collection of interlinked underground tunnels and chambers.

Setts vary in size, with multiple entrances that are dome shaped. Badgers use their powerful legs to dig out the setts and then drag bedding in for comfort and warmth. The longest Eurasian Badger sett known is 879m long, has 178 entrances and 50 chambers.

Setts can usually be found on the edges of woodland, copses and hedgerows, preferably near pastureland, though they can also be located within suburbs, farmland and abandoned quarries.

For badgers, setts are a critical resource that allow them to retreat underground during the day, shelter from adverse weather, raise their young, sleep, socialise with other clan members and keep warm during the winter.

The main sett is permanently occupied, but badgers also have annex setts, subsidiary setts and outlying setts, which are not in use all of the time. In the absence of badgers, other wildlife such as foxes, rabbits or mice may take advantage of the shelter.

Setts are passed from one generation to the next. As clans grow, so do setts, with new chambers and tunnels being dug to both accommodate new members, and to renew old tunnels and chambers which may have collapsed over time.

The construction of a badger sett not only benefits the badgers and other animals that may move in, but the movement of soil during the digging of these setts can have a positive effect on the surrounding composition of forest vegetation.

Badgers will replace old bedding with dry grass, leaves and other materials they can find. Old bedding can often be found near sett entrances, which has been dragged out for airing or discarding.

Nesting chambers are usually small, causing badgers to sleep curled up or close together for warmth, which is especially important in winter when badgers live from their fat reserves. Badgers are very clean animals, and rotate the use of their nesting chambers to give them time to freshen up and parasites to die.

Mating and cubs

Badgers become sexually mature at around the age of one, and breeding takes place year round. Female badgers have evolved a very rare reproductive ability that delays implantation by up to eleven months once an egg has been fertilised. Only 2% of mammals have this ability. This enables females to give birth in February, which is the best time of year to ensure the cubs' survival.

Pregnancy lasts seven weeks, and a sow will give birth to between 2-5 cubs.

Newborn cubs weigh between 75-130 grams and are covered in silky grey and white fur. They won't open their eyes until they are five weeks old, and rely entirely on their mother for the first 12 weeks as they depend on her milk for nutrition. At 15 weeks old the cubs will be weaned and will forage for food alone.

All badgers within a clan help to care for cubs as this increases their chances of survival. This is aided by the cubs marking themselves with the musk of the adults so they are easily recognised as clan members.

Cubs love to play-fight and chase one another, which helps their coordination and strength while also determining their place within the hierarchy of the younger clan members.

History

The earliest fossil of a badger was found in France, and is believed to be around two million years old.

Badgers have been described as the oldest land-owners in the UK, residing in these lands long before Britain became an island. 'Brock' is included in the names of many towns and villages across Britain, illustrating the presence of badgers in these ancient times.

Thousands of years ago, when bears and wolves were made extinct in the UK, the badger population would have increased dramatically as they were no longer preyed upon. Now that badgers are the largest carnivorous wild animal remaining, they are an integral species within our ecology as they help to manage the populations of other wild animals like foxes, rabbits, rats and mice.

It is believed that the word 'badger' comes from the 16th Century term 'bageard', which is believed to be due to the white stripe on top of the badger's head, referred to as a 'badge'. Badgers are also referred to as ‘brock’, which is a Celtic word meaning ‘grey’.

Badgers and humans

The badger is probably one of the most demonised protected species in the UK today, due to the volume of reported incidents that are received by organisations such as the RSPCA, League Against Cruel Sports, Naturewatch Foundation and the Badger Trust.

The various types of crime committed against badgers illustrate this, and they include:

- Sett interference
- Badger baiting
- Shooting
- Snaring and trapping
- Poisoning
- Hunting and lamping badgers with dogs (‘lamping’ is hunting at night using powerful torches or lamps)

The illegal persecution is potentially committed by a wider cross section of society than any other species, which can include person(s) from the:

- Agricultural industry
- Forestry Industry
- Developers (commercial and private)
- Householders
- Registered hunts
- Badger baiters
- People hunting and lamping with dogs

It is estimated that 50,000 badgers are also killed on the roads In Britain and this figure does not include the cubs, which die when their mothers are victims of these road deaths.

Crime

The illegal persecution of badgers is currently one of six UK Wildlife Crime Priorities and is listed due to the sheer volume of crime and intelligence amassed, rather than from an endangered species angle.

The badger in the UK is protected mainly by the Protection of Badgers Act 1992. Under this Act it is an offence to:

- Take, injure or kill a badger or attempt to do so
- Dig for a badger
- Inflict cruelty on a badger
- Possess or sell a badger
- Interfere with a badger sett whilst it is in current use

Interference with a badger sett includes:

- Damaging a sett or any part of it
- Destroying a sett
- Obstructing access to any sett or entrance

- Causing a dog to enter a sett
- Disturbing a badger whilst it is occupying its sett

Other relevant legislation, which is often applied alongside the Protection of Badgers Act 1992 are:

- The Wildlife and Countryside Act 1981
- The Hunting Act 2004
- The Animal Welfare Act 2006

Badger baiting and sett digging

Historically, hunting badgers for sport has been a common pastime in many countries. The Dachshund (German for 'badger hound') dog breed was bred for this purpose. Despite being made illegal in the UK in 1835 and badgers receiving their own protection legislation in 1973 (which was updated in 1992), badger baiting is as prevalent today as it was then.

Offenders are organised and can travel considerable distances to commit their crimes.

Sett digging and baiting is traditionally where badgers are tracked underground in their setts by terrier dogs with tracking equipment fitted. The dogs are placed down the sett to locate a badger. Once located, the men above ground dig down into the tunnels or chambers to extract the badger. This digging down is known as 'crowning down'.

Once the badger is dug out, it is either thrown to the dogs for an immediate fight (with the terriers and, in many cases, larger dogs commonly known as 'Longdogs' such as lurchers), or retained in a cage for a pre-determined fight at another location.

If the dogs don't kill the badgers, the badgers are often clubbed to death. They can also be injured with spades or knives if they're proving too strong for the dogs.

The dogs can also sustain terrible injuries and suffering, notably with injuries to their lower jaw from the badger's strong bite. Offenders don't seek professional treatment for their injured dogs to avoid detection. The dogs are treated as tools of the trade and are shown little compassion or welfare consideration.

Baiters will often keep dogs in allotments with badger baiting equipment to avoid detection at home.

Badgers are often placed at the roadside to imitate road kill, or they're buried inside dug-out setts, which are filled back up to conceal their illegal activity, which is known as 'back filling'.

Often, badger baiting is reported subsequent to the crime, and the main evidence left is the sett digging and crowning down.

Lamping badgers

Badgers are also lamped at night (hunting at night using powerful torches or lamps to highlight their target). People often trespass on land at night to do this, before releasing their dogs to chase down and kill their prey.

They use long dogs such as lurchers. The prey can also include hares, rabbits and deer.

Investigations and convictions

Investigations can be lengthy and complex, involving multiple offenders and partnership working amongst the various agencies such as the police, RSPCA, and a local badger group.

Forensic evidence is playing an ever more vital and prominent role in investigations with the use of DNA, and examination of dogs, blood, hair and devices, as their pastime or interest is often recorded on mobiles, computers and lap tops.

Courts have powers to confiscate equipment and dogs, and ban people from keeping animals. Many dogs involved in badger baiting are rehomed to safety.

Any case of badger baiting involving interference or damage to the sett will have to prove the badger sett was in current use at the time, to obtain a conviction in relation to the sett itself.

The term 'current use' is not further defined under the Protection of Badgers Act, and is therefore open to interpretation.

In the case of the Procurator Fiscal Jedburgh v Harris & McLauchlan [2010], Sherriff Drummond issued a judgement, which highlighted several items that he considered would need to be present to prove that a sett was in current use. These included:

- the presence of bedding
- latrines or dung pits containing fresh dung connected to a sett by recently used paths (a latrine is a collection of dung pits in close proximity to one another)
- pad marks identifiable as badgers entering the sett
- well used paths with pad marks evidencing use by badgers
- remnants of vegetation present in excavated soil
- hairs snagged in entrances or in freshly ejected soil or bedding
- foraging marks
- the shape of the entrance
- a freshly dug latrine pit with no dung

At least two of the above signs should be evidenced in court to prove a sett is displaying signs of current use.

Magpie facts (Maggie's page)

Folklore

Around the world, magpies hold an important place in folklore. In China, their voice is looked upon as being a harbinger of good fortune and they are believed to be a sacred symbol of joy, marital bliss and lasting fortune. So too for Koreans - the magpie is the village spirit that announces positive omens, invites good people to come and has a tiger as its servant to do its bidding. In Mongolia, the magpie even has control of the weather.

In Germany, one magpie is viewed as unlucky; two brings happiness or marriage; three implies a successful journey; four is a sign of good news, and five suggests visitors are to be expected. In France, heather and laurel are hung from tall trees to attract them, so their chatter can warn of approaching wolves. In Greece, the magpie is regarded as sacred, and is linked to the God Bacchus, the God of wine, and consequently is associated with drunkenness.

Intelligence

The Eurasian magpie is as intelligent as great apes, being capable of problem solving, tool use, making predictive judgements and feeling complex emotions, including grief. They are one of only a few non-human species that can recognise their reflection.

Magpies mimic other birds and can be trained to talk. Their cawing reflects their intensely competitive and social nature. A large gathering is referred to as a 'parliament' which can number up to one hundred.

Etymology

The 'pie' in magpie refers to the black and white or pied plumage. Originally magpies were known simply as 'the Pie', then in the 16th century the prefix Mag was added meaning 'chatterer'.

Mating and Breeding

Magpies overwinter in woods, parks, gardens and hedgerows and are a common resident throughout most of Britain. Mating takes place in spring. Pairs often remain together from one season to the next and occupy the same territory in successive years.

Clutches, laid in April, usually contain five or six eggs. They are incubated for about three weeks by the female who is fed on the nest by the male. Chicks emerge with a light covering of down and first open their eyes after a week. During this period and for several more weeks, both parents feed them and keep them safe. The chicks fledge at around 27 days.

Only one brood of chicks is reared unless the first clutch fails to survive. Typically, a third of the clutch does not live to the fledging stage and only a fifth of fledglings make it through their first year. Once past this point, magpies usually live for just under four years. The oldest recorded age for a magpie is 21 years and 8 months. This bird was ringed in Coventry in 1925, but unfortunately, was shot in 1947.

Diet

Magpies are omnivorous, taking insects, small birds, eggs, small mammals, frogs and small reptiles as well as a variety of fruits. Magpie population increases may be attributed to the burgeoning number of road kills (as a result of increased traffic), which provides carrion for the birds.

The Larsen Traps

The trap which features in Maggie's story was originally designed by a Danish gamekeeper in the 1950s and has long been banned in its country of origin. However, it is still used by the shooting industry in Britain. Although they are only meant to capture magpies and other corvids, they do also catch birds which are protected by law.

There are many rules as to the use of these traps, but since they are placed in areas which are rarely scrutinised by anyone except those who have a vested interest in the elimination of the magpies, the rules are not always followed.

Where to find further information:

1. Badgerland
   www.badgerland.co.uk

2 Wildlife Online: Natural History of Badgers
   www.bovinetb.info/docs/natural-history-of-the-european-badger.pdf

3. The Order of Bards, Ovates and Druids
   www.druidry.org/library/animals/magpies-story-seven

4. Wikipedia - Magpie
   https://en.wikipedia.org/wiki/Eurasian_magpie

5. Artist Geoff Francis - for more details of Geoff's art, writings and environmental work
   https://artistgeofffrancis.com

6. No More Dodos - an environmental charity, uniquely using Art and Sport to inspire change.
   No More Dodos has supported the production of this book
   https://www.nomoredodos.org

Naturewatch Foundation

Naturewatch Foundation is a registered charity founded in 1991, working to improve the lives of animals worldwide. A key part of their work revolves around public education to ensure animals are recognised as sentient beings capable of suffering, and full regard is always paid to their welfare requirements.

The aim of one of their campaigns is to end badger baiting, sett digging, illegal lamping, killing and other acts of cruelty towards badgers involving the use of dogs. Geoff Francis very generously offered to write this book to raise awareness of the illegal persecution of badgers to the younger generation, who are the next carers of our natural world.

About the Author

Geoff Francis is a Saatchi-shortlisted artist, sculptor, award-winning photographer, published author of fiction and non-fiction with 13 books to his credit, a film-maker and poet. A vegan for 47 years, all Geoff's work and projects have had an ethical theme at their core.

Geoff set up and ran the first paper recycling for the nascent Friends of the Earth in 1971, and Animaline for Linda McCartney, Carla Lane and Rita Tushingham in the 1980s. Geoff also has a long-term involvement with Hillside Animal Sanctuary and is a trustee of Journey's End Animal Sanctuary in Florida.

Most recently, Geoff's vision has led to his co-founding the environmental charity No More Dodos, which uniquely uses sport and art to inspire individual action for change, and to support organisations working on behalf of endangered species and habitats.

www.artistgeofffrancis.com
www.nomoredodos.org

Lightning Source UK Ltd.
Milton Keynes UK
UKHW052237210520
363608UK00004B/26